CHAOS *to* CALM

Discovering Solutions to the Everyday Problems of Living with Autism

Martha Gabler

Chaos to Calm: Discovering Solutions to the Everyday Problems of Living with Autism

For information contact:
TAGteach International LLC
7607 Taft Place
Indian Trail NC 28079
USA
TAGteach.com

Library of Congress Control Number: 2013911449

ISBN: 149041102X
ISBN 13: 978-1490411026

Editing: Jeff Palley (jeffpalley@gmail.com)
Cover/book design: Rosamond Grupp

For additional resources or to contact the author please visit AutismChaosToCalm.com

Dedication

I would like to express my thanks to Karen Pryor, Joan Orr and Theresa McKeon of TAGteach for their efforts in regards to this book, to Jeff Palley, the editor, for his patience and careful work, and to Rosamond Grupp, for her work on the cover design.

Also, my thanks to my husband Eric, our two sons, Jeffrey and Douglas, and family and friends who have helped along the way.

Foreword by Karen Pryor

I remember vividly the moment when I first heard of autism. It was in the early '60s. I was standing in our training area at Sea Life Park in Hawaii, next to one of the dolphin tanks, chatting with Gregory Bateson, the famous psychologist and philosopher who worked at the research institute next door. Gregory used the word "autism." I must have looked puzzled, because he clarified by describing some aspects of autism, including absence of language.

Children without words. I was stunned by the news, and by a simultaneous realization: we dolphin trainers could help. I carefully filed that conversation with Gregory away in my mind: autistic children. Would I ever have a chance to meet some?

Years after my career as a dolphin trainer, I wrote a book about how to use conditioned reinforcers and shaping and stimulus control and the rest of B.F. Skinner's arcane vocabulary in daily life, not just with dolphins but with one's family, in the office, in sports, and even with yourself. I wrote it with parents in mind. Alas my publishers, Simon & Schuster, gave the book a sort of jokey name, referring to the absence of punishment in this technology: *Don't Shoot the Dog.* Naturally not one parent in a thousand would pick it up. Dog owners, however, loved it: after all this was also a totally new way to train dogs.

Psychology professors also found a use for the book. They used it as a teaching text, and sometimes asked me to speak at their gatherings. In the early 90's I was attending an annual meeting of the Association for Behavior Analysis, when I got on an elevator with a group of women from a school that specialized in helping children with autism.

"Oh," I said, excited, "I've always wanted to try working with your children the way we work with dolphins." Oops. They were deeply offended by the idea that we might use a method with children that we use with animals—except for one. Myrna Libby. By the time we got off the elevator Myrna, a program director at the school, and, it turned out, a breeder of golden retrievers, had extracted a promise from me to visit the school if I ever got to Boston.

In 1998, divorced and with my family grown, I moved to Boston to be near my daughter and her growing family. I called Myrna Libby. She invited me out to the school to have a look around. "Bring clickers," she said.

The clickers Myrna was referring to were toy clickers we now used to train dogs (dog trainers didn't want to go around carrying a dolphin trainer's whistle in their teeth). The training system I'd used in my career as a dolphin trainer had proved to be a very successful way of communicating without words, with ANY learner. It was not a question of intelligence; this is the way any species with a nervous system is designed to learn good news. By finding the right marker for the species—a splash, a blink of light, a touch—you could train anything or anyone.

Today, clickers are in use with human learners of all sorts, all over the world, but in 1998 it was a new idea, and some people objected. "Clickers are for dogs, everyone knows that; how dare you use them with children?" I like the answer one behavior analyst gives to parents: "Every medicine you give to your child or take yourself was worked out first with animals. Aren't you glad we developed these techniques with animals before using them for people?"

For 18 months I spent one day a week as a consultant at the school. At the time they had 300 employees and about 200 children, mostly in residence (there are many more, today). I could see from the start that positive reinforcement was the primary tool at this school. Most of the children seemed to be content, even happy, and even those that came in with miserably bad behaviors soon improved. Under Myrna's guidance I taught teachers to be more like dolphin trainers: to ration their words, to observe emotional signals closely, and to use the powerful marker signal, usually in the form of a clicker, as well as the food treats they were already using, to reach the bodies and minds of these children.

The people whom I found heartbreaking were not the children, who seemed to be doing pretty well, but the parents. In the halls, in the lobby, in the cafeteria, I often saw parents, side by side, visiting a child already in the school, or there for consultation about bringing a child. They had done all they could, on their own. They were worn out, tired, anxious, and deep in grief. To give a child over to others is a wrenching decision. And yet living with a child with autism—well, in this book, Martha Gabler makes it very clear just what parents can go through, trying to cope, not just now and then, but day and night, year after year.

There is outside help, if you can find it—and if you can afford it. Applied behavior analysis, a method used at major autism schools, has been scientifically demonstrated to be useful and beneficial. But there is little help for the parents when a therapist is unavailable: until Martha Gabler. The Gablers are themselves parents of a very challenging non-verbal autistic son. Martha's story takes us through her own experiences, learning how to use the tools of reinforcement, step by step, to build behavior one can live with.

The wonderful thing about this technology is that once you understand the principles you can use them on your own. Martha is the poster Mom for this phenomenon. Yes, she had a book—mine; and she had some human-applications instruction in seminars led by Theresa McKeon and Joan Orr, the founders of TAGteach. But it was Martha, working on her own, who picked up the tools—the marker, the reinforcers, shaping, and cues—and made them fit her own circumstances and her own son's potential. As she shows us, the underlying deficits might not change; but the behavior, and the level of communication—those can change. And a parent can do it.

One of the gifts of reinforcement-based interaction is that it brings awareness of how things are for the learner, not just for yourself: and the outcome of that awareness is respect. How brave they can be, these children. And how funny; sometimes, concealed under the inability to communicate, there is a great sense of humor. I hope Martha Gabler's wonderful book reaches the hands of every parent with a tantruming child, every parent spending sleepless nights, every parent with a son or daughter who can't be taken to the supermarket or on a bus without stress and anxiety. May this book bring you hope. And help. And some peace. And maybe even joy.

Karen Pryor
Watertown, Massachusetts
May 20, 2013

Contents

Chapter 1

Introduction

Recently, at a sports outing for children with disabilities, I saw a sight familiar to all autism parents: the tug-of-war. A handsome, sturdy boy about 5 years old was screaming, wailing and resisting with all his strength his mother's attempts to walk him over to the activity area. These two behaviors, screaming and tugging, continued despite all the comforting and blandishments of the mother and several kind volunteers, until finally the mother abandoned the event and drove off. I could imagine her during the drive home, shaking with tears of frustration and anger after trying so hard to have her son enjoy an outdoor event.

This outcome was unnecessary. Despite his autism, that child *could* have walked quietly to the gathering point and waited for the event to start. He and his mother could have had a pleasant outing. What was missing? The child did not have two basic behaviors, which I will call "Quiet Mouth," and "Nice Walking." These are behaviors that can be taught easily and quickly with a behavioral method known as "Teaching with Acoustical Guidance" (TAGteach®), and they are the basis of learning more complex behaviors such as going to the store, sitting in waiting rooms, and taking part in everyday life.

This mother's experience took me back to my own early days with my profoundly autistic child. At age three, Doug was a spinning, shrieking, chaotic, out-of-control toddler with no words, no communication and no skills. He could not sit still for one second, he could not stand still for one second, and he could not respond to language. I refer to those times in the beginning as "the dreadful, early years." Every day, I felt as if we were drowning.

I arranged an evaluation for my son for what I assumed was a speech delay. To my horror, the therapist turned to me and asked, "Have you ever considered that your son may have autism?" That day was the first time I had the shattering experience of hearing my son's name and the word "autism" in the same sentence. I'll never forget it. Autism. One word. Six little letters. Life changed forever.

From that moment, we experienced all the agonies that autism families everywhere experience after they hear the news. I call it the triple tragedy. First, the heartbreaking diagnosis. Second, no help, even though excellent scientific methods exist to help children with autism, there are massive financial and bureaucratic obstacles to getting them. Third, no one cares. Every autism family has to deal with the pain and grief of each of these blows and come to terms with them. After a while, we realized that we were completely on our own if we were to help our child, and that we had to take action on our own. This was a terrifying moment. I had no idea that it would end up being a liberation.

By the time Doug was eight, we were physically isolated and I was absolutely desperate just to take a simple walk around the block. It was difficult to go anywhere with him because as soon as we were outside, he would race around and scream. He was very fast, and it took two people to watch him.

How do you do it? How do you work with your child if he is so chaotic that he can't sit or stand for even one second? What do you do if he can't understand your words, can't say any words, or, as Doug did, runs away shrieking when we spoke to him? What do you do to help a child who hits himself and bangs his head on the wall repeatedly? This was the dilemma we faced when we had to confront the reality of an out-of-control child with severe autism and no words.

We decided that we wanted to rely only on methods based on scientific research, primarily the science of Applied Behavior Analysis (ABA), to teach our son and deal with his many difficult and sometimes violent behaviors.

A glancing reference in a listserv post led me to Karen Pryor's book, *Don't Shoot The Dog*, and her method of positive teaching. I already had some knowledge of positive reinforcement after several years of doing ABA (Applied Behavioral Analysis) and VB (Verbal Behavior) therapy programs at home. After reading this book, I saw immediately how much more I could do to teach my child, especially to teach those elusive behaviors he needed to function in the world outside the therapy room. So I dived in.

After reading the book and attending a TAGteach seminar, I tackled the problem again, but this time, the outcome was different. I taught my son to walk with me quietly, and finally we were able to go to many more places than just the neighborhood park. Because Doug was non-verbal, I was happy to find a method of teaching that could succeed without using words for instruction or praise. As we progressed through the years Doug's ability to understand the spoken word, follow directions and accept praise improved significantly. He now understands much of what we say, but he does not verbalize well and would still be considered non-verbal.

Now, Doug is seventeen and we are in a much better place. Our son has academic skills: he can read, write, do math, formulate sentences in structured settings, and memorize poetry. His receptive language skills are excellent, but his expressive language skills are low. He loves to learn and works hard on his academics. He has good behavior skills: we can come and go with him as we please, and he is well-behaved and cooperative. He has grown into a delightful, cheerful teenager who loves life, and loves to go out and have a good time. He gives us joy every day. Our home is calm. We have a good situation with happy parents and a happy child. We still have problems, but things are much better than I could have imagined years ago.

This book focuses on how I used one particular scientifically-based method (TAGteach) to teach the behaviors that enabled us to have a better home life and get out in the community. I found that instead of struggling with my child's difficult behaviors, I could use the time to start building good behaviors. Here is how we dealt with the problems of living with autism, how we taught Doug thc complex behaviors that enabled us to have a better family life. In sum, it tells how we went from chaos to calm.

Please keep in mind that this is our personal story, based on our family's experience with our child. These are my ideas, my actions, and my thoughts as an autism parent. My story is not intended as professional advice. Parents should always seek the help of qualified professionals in the care of a child with learning or behavioral challenges. I am reporting my own experience with my own boy.

Also, I recognize that there are girls with autism and their problems are no less severe, but I hope that parents of girls will try to relate, even when I wander into more general discussions where "he or she" or "he/she" would be more appropriate in a different book. But the overwhelming majority of my personal experience with autism has been with my own son, and I wanted to make that clear. So I hope you will understand my decision to avoid awkward "he/she" wording and instead use masculine pronouns throughout this true-life account.

What is TAGteach?

As I mentioned, one of our family's requirements was that any methods we used be scientifically based, so I dug deeply into the research behind TAGteach. What I learned is that TAGteach is based on behavioral science and involves the use of positive reinforcement to achieve behavior goals. In particular, it combines positive reinforcement with an audible event marker signal.

The TAG part of TAGteach stands for Teaching with Acoustical Guidance and refers to the audible marker, a key tool used in the system that is used to highlight success. The TAGteach protocol also includes tools to deliver information, reduce inefficient language, assess performance, create confidence and deliver positive reinforcement. TAGteach is *not* a substitute for other behavioral methods used to teach children with autism, such as other forms of Applied Behavioral Analysis (ABA) or Verbal Behavior (VB) therapy, but it can serve as a very powerful accompaniment to these methods as well as other methods used in teaching children with autism.

It is *not* a cure for autism. But it is a teaching method that was uniquely successful at reaching our severely autistic and profoundly nonverbal child.

How does TAGteach Work?

TAGteach combines positive reinforcement with an event marker signal, often an acoustical signal. Many things can be used to "mark" an event. I used box clickers, flashlights, and even handclaps if I had nothing else available. People use ballpoint pens (the top makes a click-like sound when pressed down), tally counters, and even the "cricket clickers" available at novelty stores. The marker—the key communication tool used in the system—makes a distinctive "click" sound to *mark* a behavior at the time it occurs. This sound becomes a simple acoustical message that is quickly processed. The benefit is that it is binary, with only two values: The mark means YES, and absence of the mark means "try again." The mark is the critical information that learners need to acquire new skills.

As soon as I read about this, it made instant sense to me. My son was so chaotic and averse to verbal coaching that I could immediately see how the event marker could do what my words (or begging and pleading) could not. He was one of those kids who always ran around with his fingers in his ears. He could not endure listening to words, and the quickest way to make him bolt was to start talking to him. The event marker, the "click," would tell him that what he did was good. I thought, "Wow, I can teach him without words. Wonderful!"

But I had to figure out how to apply it. To teach a skill, the first step is to identify precisely the behavior I want to increase (or technically speaking, to "reinforce"). In the case of the handsome little fellow described above, the mother could, as I did, teach Quiet Mouth behavior. The first step is to ignore, pay no attention to, and not react at all to any screaming, wailing, or crying behaviors. The next step is to watch and wait for a Quiet Mouth moment (which might only be a split second), quickly press the marker to signal success, and immediately give the child a treat to reinforce that behavior. The treat could be anything the child likes: candy, pretzel pieces, a chance to squeeze a soft, plushy object. The final step is to repeat this *mark-then-reinforce* behavior with every Quiet Mouth moment throughout the day and for the next weeks. When I used this approach with Doug, I started to see a reduction in screaming and wailing and an increase in Quiet Mouth behaviors.

Technical Terminology

In the above paragraph, I use the words "positive reinforcement," "reinforce," and "reinforcers." These are technical terms that have specific meanings. So below, courtesy of Karen Pryor's book, *Don't Shoot the Dog,* is a brief description of those terms. I found that once I had a basic understanding of these terms, it was easier for me to teach Doug.

Definition of "reinforcement"

"Scientifically speaking, reinforcement is an event that (a) occurs during or upon completion of a behavior, and (b) increases the likelihood of that behavior occurring in the future. The key elements here are two: the two events are connected in real time—the behavior engenders the reinforcement—and then the behavior occurs more frequently."

Definition of "reinforcer"

"A reinforcer is something that *increases* a behavior . . . ". It can be a small piece of candy, a chance to play with a desired toy, or, for more advanced learners, a token that can be collected and traded in for special treats or privileges (TV or computer time, going to the movies, pizza, or money). A reinforcer must be something that the child values and is willing to work for.

Definition of "shaping"

Shaping is a process by which a teacher reinforces behavior in a way that incrementally changes the starting behavior into the finished behavior. So when I describe changing a behavior step by step so that each step is a little closer to the final goal, this is shaping behavior. Our children with autism cannot make behavior changes in big chunks, we must break the behavior down and build it up with small changes so that they always have success along the way. Sometimes I may be tempted to make a big jump in teaching a behavior, because things are going so well. It is better to resist this temptation and move ahead in small steps. This way, if the behavior falls apart (the child is tired, there is a new environment, there is a new teacher, any number of other factors are upsetting the child), there is a point of success to go back to, that I have already taught and reinforced. If I didn't reinforce those small incremental improvements, I will end up going back to the very beginning when, inevitably, something conspires to cause my child to regress.

Why use positive reinforcement to teach a behavior?

The use of positive reinforcement to increase desired behaviors is recommended for helping people with autism. Here is what autism research organizations and government agencies have to say:

The Organization for Autism Research states:

> Interventions based upon the principles of applied behavior analysis (ABA) have been documented as highly effective in teaching a range of academic, social, communicative, motor, and adaptive skills. The central theory behind ABA is that "Behavior rewarded (reinforced) is more likely to be repeated than behavior ignored." Behavioral intervention seems to help children "learn to learn." Research has shown that interventions based upon the principles of ABA consistently teach new skills and behaviors to children with autism.

The Association for Science in Autism Treatment states:

> Many studies show that ABA is effective in increasing behaviors and teaching new skills (Goldstein 2002, Odom et al. 2003, McConnell 2002). In addition, many studies demonstrate that ABA is effective in reducing problem behavior (Horner et al., 2002). A number of studies also indicate that, when implemented intensively (more than 20 hours per week) and early in life (beginning prior to the age of 4 years), ABA may produce large gains in development and reductions in the need for special services (Smith, 1999).

The United States Surgeon General (1999) concluded that:

> Thirty years of research demonstrated the efficacy of applied behavioral methods in reducing inappropriate behavior and in increasing communication, learning and appropriate social

> behavior *(Association for Science in Autism Treatment. Autism Treatments: Descriptions and Research Summaries. Summaries of Scientific Research on Interventions in Autism: Applied Behavior Analysis, 2011).*

From the International Encyclopedia of Education, 1988:

> Research has shown that the most effective way to reduce problem behavior in children is to strengthen desirable behavior through positive reinforcement rather than trying to weaken undesirable behavior by using aversive or negative processes *(Bijou, S. W. The International Encyclopedia of Education, 1988. Parenting Prescriptions. Correcting Undesirable Behavior, 2011).*

Why add an audible marker?

My next questions were: We know that positive reinforcement works, so why add an audible marker? Why not just give the treat or other reinforcer directly? While it may seem odd to "mark" a behavior with an audible marker, I realized it is common in our daily lives. Think of how many audible markers we use that we don't even notice: alarm clocks, microwave oven beeps, doorbells, telephone rings, "you've got mail" bleeps on computer email systems, fire alarms and so forth. We purposely embed audible markers in our environment because they provide vital information. That is exactly the role of the event marker for a child with autism: it teaches him, "Hey, that thing I just did is a good thing to do because I heard the sound and got a treat" and it teaches the child without burdening him with our emotion-laden voices, words, or other unhelpful sensory input.

What about a child's sensory issues?

This was another question I had. Countless articles, specialists and parents point out that children with autism can have sensory issues. For example, they may be extremely sensitive to their physical environments, especially to light, sound, activity, temperature, even changes in air pressure. I would add duration of time to this list. This heightened sensitivity is generally considered an obstacle to learning, because the child is so focused on coping with these sensations that he cannot focus on learning. In my experience, the event marker, either audible sound or a flash of light, gets around these sensory problems. It gave Doug information and guidance in small bits and with the pleasant reinforcers. My experience was that TAGteach worked well *because* of the super-sensitivity of the child with autism, not in spite of it. So, at last, I had stumbled upon a teaching method that worked *with* what is normally regarded as a problem that many children with autism have. The sensory issues that I had always regarded as a negative now became a positive. I saw my sensitive, sensory and perceptive child change and learn new behaviors as soon as I made his environment more understandable, by providing specific information and specific reinforcement. And I didn't have to say a word.

Also, because it is light, portable and flexible, TAGteach turned out to be an outstanding method for teaching behavior away from formal, structured settings. I found it to be ideal for teaching in the natural environment, and for teaching those behaviors that families need in order to take their children out in the community. I was finally able to teach my son simple skills that are the components of more complex behaviors such as:

- Going for a walk
- Getting from the front door to the car

- Getting in the car
- Behaving properly in the car
- Getting out of the car
- Walking safely through parking lots
- Walking through a grocery store
- Waiting in line at the grocery store, pharmacy, post office, bank
- Going to the park and playground
- Waiting in doctors' waiting rooms

"Just the facts, ma'am"

We've all heard that phrase, and "just the facts" is what I deliver when I "mark" a behavior. Marking a behavior requires no words, verbal explanations or lengthy demonstrations, so it was wonderfully appropriate for my son, who was profoundly nonverbal. Doug, like many children with autism, lives "in the moment," and reacts to everything that is going on in that moment. I had long observed that a lot of talking, gesturing, even comforting behavior by adults, no matter how well-intentioned, could be upsetting for him. With a single click or flash of light, the event marker delivers "just the facts." It eliminates the sensory/emotional issues of noise, and imposes no verbal requirements. Once my child hears the mark, there is nothing more required of him except to enjoy the treat. The mark provides focus and immediate feedback in a way that is pleasing, understandable and useful to my child with autism.

Karen Pryor, author of *Don't Shoot the Dog*, has written a beautiful description of why an audible sound is much better at "marking" a behavior than our spoken words:

> . . . please note that the human voice is a very poor marker signal . . . too long, too slow, too variable, carrying too many confounding messages (your sex, your age, your mood, your health, etc.) and it's also almost always late. Furthermore, you can't distinguish when you are a mini-second late with your voice, but you CAN tell at once, without experience, when your click is late *(Karen Pryor, Penn State Listserv System. Standard Celeration Society, 18 May 2005.)*

How long did it take for Doug to learn a skill?

Naturally I was curious about this, and I found out that, like all things, it depends on what I am teaching and, most important, how intensely I work with him. Certain skills, like Quiet Voice and Nice Walking went quickly. Other skills, like learning to wait, took longer. General good advice is that it will take the most time to teach the first three tag points. A tag point™ is the specific aspect of a behavior that will receive the audible reinforcing mark. Once a child has learned the cues for three tag points and can perform them reliably, the ones that follow can be learned more quickly. I started with simpler tag points first, and found Quiet Mouth easy to teach first. Another simple one to teach was Two Steps in Same Direction, part of our Nice Walking program. The play skill, Bounces Ball also went quickly. "Quickly" for us means anything from eight minutes to six months. Once I was comfortable with the basic "mark and reinforce" procedure and had fine-tuned my observation skills, most of my projects went smoothly.

How Much Does It Cost?

Expense is almost always a huge issue for autism families. Fortunately, the financial costs of doing TAGteach are minimal. Box clickers, flashlights and ball point pens are inexpensive, and people generally have these items lying around the house. Treats for the child are items most families also have around the house such as candy, pretzel pieces, fuzzy toys, or access to the computer. The book that got me interested in using a positive reinforcement-based approach, *Don't Shoot the Dog! The New Art of Teaching and Training*, is widely available and costs less than $25.

The big cost is in time and effort. Autism parents bear a crushing burden. First and foremost is the tragedy of the diagnosis. Second, while parents are reeling from this tragedy, they try to get services for their child—a daunting task because the services available are often low-intensity and poor quality. Third, while trying to work their way through the service delivery and special education quagmire, parents have to deal with the extremely difficult and disruptive behaviors of their child with little guidance or support. Children with autism can be so loud, wild and chaotic that parents cannot even get to the grocery store. Parents cannot buy food, fix dinner or eat. They cannot sleep because the child is often up all night. The family becomes exhausted, physically marooned and socially isolated. Siblings suffer, careers falter, and marriages shatter under the strain. Autism takes a terrible toll in ways that are invisible to outsiders.

Autism families are frequently advised to hire a Board Certified Behavior Analyst (BCBA) to help them deal with their children's difficult behaviors. BCBAs are trained in the science of Applied Behavior Analysis and are skilled at analyzing a child's behaviors, determining the functions of the behaviors, and setting up behavior plans for the family. This would be wonderful ... if all autism families could get ongoing help from these experienced and dedicated practitioners, but in reality, it is not possible. At the time I write this, only about half of the states require health insurance companies to provide ABA. Even if a state requires health insurance companies to provide coverage, there may not be enough practitioners to meet the demand, so families face long waiting lists. Even when there is some insurance coverage, the high deductibles, high co-pays, and high transportation expenses make the cost too much for many families, especially in the current economic climate. When it comes down to reality, most autism families are on their own in dealing with the nightmarish behaviors their children display.

When I teach my child with autism, it is enormously helpful that I have knowledge of the use of positive reinforcement to build skills. The beauty of the TAGteach method is that it takes a body of scientific knowledge and simplifies the teaching protocols to the point where non-experts can implement them, including grieving, distracted, overwhelmed autism parents, as I was then and as you may be now. Not only is TAGteach remarkably compatible with the child, as mentioned above, it works very well for the parents. Every autism parent I've ever met is an incredibly vigilant, detailed observer of their child's behaviors. Every autism parent I've ever met has told me of those beautiful fleeting moments when their child did something really great. We parents would love to see more of those great moments. Armed with a box clicker, the split second you see one of those wonderful moments, you can mark and reinforce that flash of great eye contact, understanding or interaction. When you reinforce a behavior, it will happen more often. It's easy, quick and effective. Naturally, as with everything relating to autism, I had to observe Doug, monitor his progress and make adaptations. As we in the autism community well know, each child is different, each family is different, and each environment is different.

I arranged the chapters in this book to describe what I think would be a logical progression of skills to learn. Our personal experience was more helter-skelter, and later, I often thought, "If I knew then what I know now, I would have done this or that more effectively." The next chapter starts with what I found to be the single, relatively easy task of teaching Quiet Mouth behavior. Then I progress to the more complex but very essential skill of Nice Walking. Once we have Quiet Mouth and Nice Walking behavior established, we can take these two behaviors and apply them to new settings, such as the park, playground, and grocery store. The next steps are to increase calm behaviors, reduce unwanted behaviors, manage tantrums, teach some play skills, improve communication ... and get some sleep.

Chapter 2

Quiet Mouth

Before I describe how I taught our son Quiet Mouth, I would like to expand upon a few points. First, let us discuss exactly what a "behavior" is. There is a simple, helpful definition in Dr. Martin Kozloff's book *Educating Children with Learning and Behavior Problems*. He explains:

> . . . *behavior is movement*. The two are the same thing. Whenever we use the word "behavior," we are talking about movements of the body.

If my child in engaging in a "behavior," he is "moving" something. If a child is wailing and crying, he is moving vocal chords and facial muscles. The child is not "going nuts" or "driving me crazy," which, although true from the parents' point of view, is not technically the case! The child is simply moving certain body parts, with a result that we don't like. Once I had this concept clear in my mind, I was able to figure out how to reduce the unwanted movements (vocal chords and facial muscles) and increase desirable movements, noting that in this case the good movements may seem like *lack* of movements in vocal chords and facial muscles, or appropriate vocalizations.

Crying, Screaming and Wailing

My approach for reducing crying, screaming and wailing was to ignore the wailing, wait for Quiet Mouth, mark and reinforce immediately, and repeat until Quiet Mouth was an established behavior. Specifically, I waited for the vocal chords to stop moving, immediately marked that microsecond of silence, gave a treat ("reinforcer") to my child, then waited for the vocal chords to stop moving again. Just to review, a reinforcer is anything I give a child that causes the desired behavior to increase, so the treat I give my child must be pleasing to him. If the behavior does not increase, the reinforcer didn't work, so I must find something to give him that *is* a treat.

Since I was marking and reinforcing Quiet Mouth, one would refer to Quiet Mouth as the "tag point." The tag point is a description of the precise aspect of the behavior we wish to increase. A tag point has four criteria:

1. What I Want
2. One Criterion
3. Observable
4. Five Words or Less

To keep tag points simple and observable, it is best to name them using as few words as possible. The tag point should be something that the child is physically capable of doing. This is referred to as the "point of success." I always start a teaching session with a point of success, so that my child will win right off the bat and I can build on success to get more success. If he cannot (or will not) do what I ask, the process will quickly become frustrating for everyone. I want my child to be able to perform the tag point so he experiences a lot of success right away. The value of working through the criteria for a tag point, is that it forces me to think carefully about what his current behavior looks like (what "movements" he is making), the components of the behavior I want to increase, and which of his physical movements I could target for reinforcement. Let's look at these criteria for the Quiet Mouth tag point:

1. **What I Want:** Quiet Mouth.
2. **One Criterion**: YES. Quiet Mouth.
3. **Observable**: YES. I can hear (and see) when the child stops screaming and has a Quiet Mouth. I could also count how many instances of Quiet Mouth occurred in a period of five or ten minutes.
4. **Five Words or Less:** YES. Quiet Mouth is two words.

Once the tag point of Quiet Mouth was carefully defined, I got to work. In our situation, I did not use words to describe this desired behavior to Doug. TAGteach practitioners spend a great deal of effort analyzing and breaking down a behavior or skill to define a tag point carefully; the goal is to deliver the instruction for a desired action to a learner with a specific phrase. For example, an instructor may say, "The tag point is…Touch Nose."

Or, "The tag point is…Hands on Knees." The careful verbal phrasing of the tag point is a wonderful feature for learners who have language and can use and understand words. It allows the learner to concentrate on just that single task and achieve success. Verbalizing the tag point is also a good focusing exercise for the parent, as long as the child does not react negatively to words. My son did not have the words and language skills to do this when we first started out with TAGteach. Even more, with his aversion to spoken language, using words was counterproductive. I relied completely on observing Doug and marking and reinforcing the desired physical movement. This worked very well. In fact, it worked better than I could have imagined. Accordingly, the tag points as I describe them in this book are not written as verbal instructions; they are written to describe physical movements that someone could observe and then mark and reinforce.

But back to Quiet Mouth: when I was in a room with my child and suddenly, for a split second, he stopped wailing, I instantly marked the behavior (pressed box clicker to make sound), then reinforced it (offered my child a small treat).

Then what? I waited for the desired behavior to occur again. While it might have been possible to do other things (tidy up, etc.) while waiting for a behavior to reoccur, I found it was best to set other things aside, spend the time with Doug, and concentrate on reinforcing Quiet Mouth.

How often did I mark the behavior? *Every time the behavior occurs*. I wanted my child to learn that every time he demonstrated Quiet Mouth, a treat was forthcoming! Doug quickly figured out that Quiet Mouth was a great thing to do to get treats, praise and attention from Mom, so he started offering more of this behavior. My first experience with marking Doug for Quiet Mouth ended up being hilarious. He was sitting on a big bouncy ball yowling and shrieking. Without saying a word, I sat down near him and started marking and reinforcing Quiet Mouth. Within eight minutes, he was bouncing silently on the ball, looking intently into my face with his *lips pursed together* as though to show me, "Look Ma, Quiet Mouth!" Pretty quick learning, and all without words!

But, back to technicalities. When marking and reinforcing a specific behavior even if that behavior is very rare, I am setting the stage for that behavior to increase. Karen Pryor explains:

> ***Behavior that is already occurring, no matter how sporadically, can always be intensified by positive reinforcement.***

Now, to keep that desired behavior on the increase, I must mark and reinforce it every time it occurs. The rate at which I tag and treat a behavior is called the "reinforcement schedule," another technical term. So let's discuss reinforcement schedules.

Reinforcement Schedules

There are several rates at which I was able to mark and reinforce behavior. When I was teaching Doug a behavior like Quiet Mouth and I marked and reinforced it *every* time it occurred, I was using a "continuous reinforcement schedule." A continuous reinforcement schedule is how to build, or *increase*, a desired behavior.

Once Doug was performing the desired behavior reliably, I changed to a less frequent schedule of reinforcement. The next schedule is called a "variable" schedule. This means that I will now reinforce Quiet Mouth every once in a while, maybe every other time the child does it, then every third time, then every fourth time, and finally I will reinforce at random intervals. Also, I can change from reinforcing the behavior with a candy, to reinforcing with praise and attention. At this point the behavior will be occurring often. There is a detailed discussion of reinforcement schedules in Karen Pryor's book *Don't Shoot the Dog* (pages 20-25).

When I first started reading about reinforcement schedules I felt overwhelmed and confused. Finally, an idea popped into mind that made the concept of reinforcement schedules fall into place: a comparison to building and maintaining a house. If I am building a house, I must nail down every board and fasten every door and window. If I don't fasten every single piece, I will have problems: big holes in the walls or a roof that falls down. The rules are the same when I am building a behavior: just as every part of the house must be fastened into place, so every instance of the desired behavior should be marked and reinforced every time it occurs. Once the house is built, I don't continue fastening things into place, instead I switch to maintenance work: I clean inside and keep the yard trimmed outside; I check to make sure that everything is working properly, and if not, we make repairs. It is the same with a behavior. Once the behavior is built, I monitor and reinforce it occasionally to keep it in good shape. When teaching Doug a behavior, I think about the stage we are in: if we are building a behavior, I reinforce it every time. If we are maintaining a behavior that he has mastered, I reinforce it occasionally and check to make sure he is still performing it.

It's important to add one final warning: many times people think that by "rewarding" children for behavior they should be doing anyway, they are "spoiling" the child. Yes, children should behave appropriately, and so forth, but with autism, often the child does not know what behavior he should be performing, probably cannot perform the desired behavior, or cannot maintain the behavior for any length of time. It is not the child's fault. Despite the difficulty of teaching a child with autism, oftentimes the only tools well-meaning adults have to change the child's behavior are aversive tools: repeating the request, escalating the demands, threats, punishments, and finally, blaming the learner. Result? The child shuts down and no one learns. The science of Applied Behavior Analysis and the positive reinforcement of good behaviors offer a much happier and more productive alternative: a gentle, patient method of building behaviors, where the child (a) learns precisely what we want him to do, (b) learns when we want him to do it, and (c) learns to produce this behavior for longer and longer periods of time. So, I don't hesitate to mark and reinforce when building a behavior. Children with autism have to work very hard to learn new behaviors; they deserve to be rewarded. Reinforcing a behavior is never bad, while punishment is painful and distasteful for all concerned, and can have adverse long-term consequences.

Final Step: Cues

My son could finally do Quiet Mouth and keep it up for several minutes at a stretch. That was great! Now, I wanted him to produce that behavior "on cue." That means that if I was talking on the phone and Doug started to wail, I would be able to say or indicate that I wanted Quiet Mouth behavior, and he would do it. The way I did this was to introduce a "cue" for the behavior.

A "cue" serves as an indicator to a child to perform a certain behavior, and can be either a gesture or a word. I found that a good cue for Quiet Mouth was the "shh" gesture we all make, with the index finger on our lips while saying "shh." I started introducing the "shh" gesture to Doug *while* I was reinforcing Quiet Mouth. This was a pretty natural thing to do because they go together. Doug did Quiet Mouth; I marked and did "shh," then gave him a reinforcer (treat). Pretty soon, Doug associated

Quiet Mouth and "shh." After a while, I did the "shh" gesture *first* and to see if he did Quiet Mouth. When he did Quiet Mouth, I felt like a winner! If he didn't, we kept practicing. I continued tagging Quiet Mouth, shhing and reinforcing, and soon Doug could keep quiet when I needed him to do that.

Extinction Burst

But watch out—an undesirable behavior may *increase* before it decreases! Be aware of this phenomenon. For the sake of discussion, let's say the sweet mother of the determined lad at the sports outing decides to start marking and reinforcing her child for Quiet Mouth. They are in a room together where she ignores and does not react to screaming and crying, and starts waiting for a Quiet Mouth moment. Suddenly she notices her son is screaming more than ever! It is louder and more ferocious! What's going on?

Well, let's look at the history of this behavior. Let's say that her son has usually experienced the following chain of events: he cries or wails, mother comes and holds his hand, pats his shoulder and makes comforting gestures; he cries more and gets more soothing and attention. Inadvertently, this caring mother has strengthened ("reinforced") crying behavior. Now all of a sudden he finds that he is crying, but he is *not* getting soothing attention! Being a bright and persistent little fellow, he immediately decides that he has to wail more and scream louder, so he increases the volume and intensity. However, his mother now has the knowledge and skills to manage this. She knows that this increase in crying behavior is to be expected and it is called an "extinction burst." In other words, his bad behavior is going to occur more often precisely when it is about to be extinguished. Even though it sounds and looks terrible, the extinction burst can be taken as a good sign, because it means the unwanted behavior is on the path to extinction.

The challenge is to wait out the extinction burst. This may take a few minutes, a few hours or a few days, and is the crucial time when a *parent should not give up, but should keep going.* The boy has a right to be upset. A prized reinforcer (mother's attention) has suddenly disappeared; he is only trying to get it back. His mother waits out the extinction burst, even though the crying and wailing sound ferocious. She sticks to her plan and consistently marks and reinforces each and every instance of Quiet Mouth. Some days later she notices that the house is quieter, the child is quieter, and things feel better. The cute little fellow has learned that Quiet Mouth gets him attention, praise and treats: no use keeping up the screaming and hollering because it doesn't pay off anymore.

The mother keeps going, starts adding the "shh" gesture during the mark and reinforce process, and one day she is able to say and gesture to her son, "shh" and he delivers Quiet Mouth behavior. Success! From then on she will mark and reinforce Quiet Mouth behavior at a variable rate (see discussion above).

The child and mother have *both* learned. The child has learned a useful behavior, and his mother has learned that she can skillfully teach a desired behavior to her son.

Verbal Stimming

Many children with autism engage in self-stimulatory verbal behavior, which is generally referred to as "verbal stimming." The child hums, beeps, buzzes or drones a particular sound, or series of sounds or words, over and over again. It drives parents crazy. During the early years, Doug spent a lot of time running around and saying, "Deeee, deeee, deee," over and over. We couldn't stand it, tried to quiet him down or change it, but with no luck. All we could do was shriek, "Stop deeeing!" Not very effective. If I could do it over, I would approach the problem as follows.

For me, the first part of the solution to verbal stimming was teaching Quiet Mouth, as described above. Next, we don't want to silence the child, in fact, we would like to expand the child's vocal range, so I set a second tag point called Good Sound/Word.

Let's look at the four criteria for the tag point Good Sound/Word:

1. **What I Want:** Doug utters an appropriate word or sound.

2. **One Criterion:** YES. I can mark and reinforce any appropriate word or sound other than the sound(s) of the verbal stim, and this could include sneezing, coughing, laughing, as long as the sound is different from the verbal stim.

3. **Observable**: YES. I can hear when Doug makes an appropriate sound or word that is different from the verbal stim. I could also count how many instances of Good Sound/Word occur in a period of five or ten minutes.

4. **Five Words or Less:** YES. Good Sound/Word is three words.

Reinforcing appropriate vocalizations can help decrease verbal stimming and increase other sounds and words in a child's repertoire. As always with autism, it is important to observe a child's behavior and responses and make adaptations as necessary to each unique situation.

I refer to these skills, Quiet Mouth and Good Sound/Word, as the two components of Nice Voice behavior. Nice Voice is a helpful skill which we combined with other skills to improve the happiness and mobility of our family.

Quick Summary of the TAGteach Process

I have introduced quite a few concepts during the Quiet Mouth example that was the subject of this chapter. I think it is useful to summarize my TAGteach tactics here as a quick review and as a point of reference that you can use when creating your own plans for teaching behaviors that are not spelled out in this book.

1) I define the final goal behavior in terms of what I want (for example: "I want Doug to put on his boots" – as opposed to "I want Doug to stop running outside in his socks in the rain"). The goal must be phrased in the positive to describe what I want.

2) I think about the component parts of the behavior and break it down into the smallest parts I can, trying to focus on the muscle movements that will create the behavior (this will become clearer as we move through the examples in this book).

3) I assess Doug's abilities and come up with a starting point. For every new teaching session, I always start with a point of success. This is something that I know he can already do and so he is pretty much guaranteed to get a tag right away. This ensures that we start off each session with immediate success. Usually I choose a point of success that Doug demonstrated

near the middle or toward the end of the previous teaching session (but not the very last thing that he accomplished in the previous session). This way I avoid starting with something he may have struggled with and that might frustrate him.

4) Once I have identified the point of success, I formulate this as a tag point. The tag point is the specific behavior that can earn Doug a tag when he accomplishes it. This must meet the four tag point criteria:

    1. **What I Want**
    2. **One Criterion**
    3. **Observable/Measurable**
    4. **Five Words or Less**

5) I change the tag point criteria slowly, in tiny increments, so that Doug is always moving forward towards the final goal. For example, my goal might be to have five seconds of Quiet Mouth. I would start with a fleeting moment, because at first, that is all that Doug can give me. In fact, even if the fleeting moment is only caused by him taking a breath, I tag that. I gradually increase the duration by a fraction of a second, then one second, then two seconds etc. Sometimes I go back to a shorter duration, just so that it is not becoming endlessly

more difficult from him to earn his tag. This incremental building of a behavior is called shaping and it is as much art as it is science. I found that I became more skilled at this along with my child.

6) I give the treat every time I mark a behavior, even if my child starts back up with an undesirable behavior before I have the chance to hand him a treat. The child must be able to trust that when he hears the click sound he will get a treat. If he is too upset to take the treat, I just set it on the table in his view, for later.

7) I am always aware of the "three try rule." If Doug has tried three times in a row without success, I go back to a previous point of success. This is more of a guideline than a rule. I very carefully watch Doug's body language and facial expressions. If I notice signs of frustration, or I know that we are working on something difficult, I might go back to a point of success after one failure. There is nothing to gain in creating frustration for either of us.

8) I end each teaching session on a note of success. It is always best to stop while a child is still enjoying the session and is cooperating, rather than pushing on to the actual point of failure and ending with frustration or worse, a tantrum. If I have to relax my criteria to something very easy, just so that he will win on the last trial, that is what I will do. Then I will remind myself to stop sooner the next time.

There are also some rules that I established for myself after much trial and error, and I list them here so that you can adopt them as well and benefit from my experience without having too much of the error part:

Rule #1: Only ask my child to do what he is capable of doing.

Rule #2: Only ask my child to do something for the length of time that he is capable of doing it.

Rule #3: Monitor his emotional reactions carefully.

Rule #4: Mark and reinforce lavishly all good behaviors.

Rule #5: Reinforce every time I mark a behavior (regardless of whatever subsequent behavior is occurring).

Chapter 3

Going For a Walk

The solution I discovered for building good walking behaviors was to teach the following four skills:

1. Two Steps in Same Direction
2. Walk Beside Me
3. Feet on Ground
4. Stand/Wait

What I wanted was for my child to walk calmly with us wherever we needed to go, and to respond to three cues: "Walk Beside Me," "Stop," and "Wait."

Nice walking behavior is a vital skill for a child with autism to master because so much that we do requires some type of walking. A child should be able to walk to the car, walk safely through the parking lot to the store, walk around in the store, walk in the park, walk around the block, and do all of these different types of walking without tantrums, screaming or running away: a tall order for a kid with autism.

In addition to safety, walking has huge health benefits. Many kids with autism do not get enough exercise, and walking is a simple, inexpensive activity that a family can do almost anywhere. Plus, once a child is a skilled walker, the whole family can go out and enjoy the natural environment. Even though it takes time, it is a valuable skill to teach.

Doug was extremely difficult to manage outside. Even in the backyard, we had to keep our eyes on him constantly and always stay within three feet of him because we never knew when he would dash off or to where. If he was not dashing off, he would hang on my shoulder or arm so heavily that I was almost carrying him. I tried and failed many times to teach him to walk nicely.

After learning about TAGteach I decided to try again. I analyzed his walking behavior and observed that he could not walk in a straight line. He would take one step, dart off in any one of several different directions, take another step, dart off, and so on—very difficult to manage and very dangerous in the street. I felt like a lion in the bush, constantly waiting to pounce and dash to catch him. Sometimes he would take one step and spin, sometimes three or four steps before he would spin and dart. To keep him safe I had to circle around him constantly and stay within arm's length.

Walking Tag Points

Walking tag point #1: Same Direction

After this observation, I went through the process of deciding what to identify, mark and reinforce. I decided that my first tag point would be Two Steps in Same Direction. I watched Doug's feet: if his first step was in one direction, I waited to see if the second footstep was in the same direction. If it was in the same direction, I marked the behavior. If not, I waited to see what the next step would look like. With my event marker (a box clicker) I could provide very specific information to him: when his second footstep hit the ground in the same direction as the first, he earned a tag and a treat. Here are the criteria for the tag point, Two Steps in Same Direction.

1. **What I Want:** Doug takes two (or more) steps in the same direction.

2. **One Criterion:** YES. I can tag the second step in the same direction.

3. **Observable**: YES. I can see when he takes two steps in the same direction. I could also count how many instances of Two Steps in Same Direction occurred in a period of five or ten minutes.

4. **Five Words or Less:** YES. Two Steps in Same Direction is five words.

Armed with my box clicker and a pocketful of fruit roll-ups, I took Doug into the street and started walking and shaping the behavior of moving in a consistent direction. Every time, by chance, that he took two steps in the same direction, I marked and reinforced the behavior. Soon he was doing Two Steps in Same Direction consistently, so I changed the tag point to Three Steps in Same Direction. Before I knew it, the tag point was Four Steps in Same Direction, then Five Steps in Same Direction, and by then we were able to do nice walks around the block. Success! At that point I changed the reinforcement schedule: I no longer marked each and every set of five steps (continuous reinforcement), but I varied it: sometimes I marked/reinforced after three steps, ten steps, or twenty steps (variable reinforcement). Within six months I was able to take him, not only for long walks around the neighborhood, but on five mile hikes with a local hiking club. Both Doug and I were able to enjoy these outings and he continues to like to hike.

Walking tag point #2: Walk Beside Me

While walking in a consistent direction was great, walking has several other component skills that Doug needed to learn: keeping pace with us, stopping on cue, and standing still and waiting. I wanted my child's walking pace to be about the same as the mine (naturally, when Doug was small, I would moderate my pace to his ability). It's no good to be chasing after him or to have him lagging behind. After going through the identify, mark and reinforce process, I set a new tag point, Walk Beside Me. I decided to mark and reinforce my son every time he walked beside me within arm's length. Here is the criteria analysis for the Walk Beside Me tag point:

1. **What I Want**: Doug walks beside me.
2. **One Criterion:** YES. I can mark when Doug walks beside me.

3. **Observable:** YES. I can see when Doug walks beside me.

4. **Five Words or Less**: YES. Walk Beside Me is three words.

So, I marked and reinforced Walk Beside Me and it worked well to keep Doug close by. Since he learned this behavior quickly, I decided to work on a cue. I wanted to be able to indicate to him, even if he was at a distance, to come over and walk beside me. The cue I decided to use was a gesture: waving my left hand next to my leg. From then on, whenever I marked him for Walk Beside Me, I made sure to wave my left hand and then reinforce. Slowly, I was able to move the cue up, so that I could wave my left hand and he would come to me to walk. This also went fairly quickly and smoothly. Walk Beside Me served as a "value added tag point" meaning that it captured the behavior being tagged and also taught my child to come to me when I waved my hand. So I got two behaviors for the price of one. I hadn't realized that when I started, but it was a nice bonus.

Walk Beside Me is an invaluable skill for us and we use it in many settings. Since it is so important, I really praise Doug for keeping pace, and I reinforce it frequently so that it remains a strong, reliable behavior. It took some time and practice for Doug and I to keep pace together at a rate that was comfortable for both of us. Also, the pace changed over time, as he grew and could take bigger steps. Like many kids with autism, he also had the occasional tendency to bolt, so it was important to keep an eye out for telltale signs of bolting. My son's muscles tense up in a certain way prior to bolting, and as soon as I saw that I swung my arm up in front of his chest to prevent it. I then gave him extra treats for Walk Beside Me behavior. While it can still happen, bolting now is a rare behavior.

Walking tag point #3: Two Feet on Ground (stop)

The final two tag points for Nice Walking are Feet on Ground (Stop) and Stand/Wait.

Why these two skills? Sometimes it is necessary to stop at corners or for a red light. When we stop, we usually have both feet on the ground, so the tag point I decided to mark and reinforce was Feet on Ground. Let's analyze the criteria for the tag point Feet on Ground.

1. **What I Want**: Doug stops at corners, crosswalks, or wherever necessary.

2. **One Criterion:** Yes. Tag point is Feet on Ground.

3. **Observable:** YES. I can see when Doug stops walking and has both feet on the ground. I could also count how many instances of Feet on Ground occurred in a period of five or ten minutes.

4. **Five Words or Less:** YES. Feet on Ground is three words.

To teach Feet on Ground, I observed Doug when we were out walking. Whenever he stopped with both feet on the ground, I marked and reinforced. Since I was building this behavior, I marked and reinforced every time I saw it. Doug soon increased his "stopping" behavior. To add a cue, I said the word "stop" whenever he stopped. I took pains to say, "Stop," in a happy, praising way to show that I was pleased with the stopping behavior. When I could reliably say, "Stop," to Doug and he halted with both feet on the ground, I breathed a sigh of relief. To be able to shout to my child, "Stop," if he is running into the street or down an aisle in a store, and to know that he will actually stop, is a wonderful feeling. It made me feel confident about taking Doug on outings. Since "stop" is such an important behavior, it is important to monitor it closely and reinforce it often.

I also learned that it was important not to get mad or upset on those occasions when he did bolt. Usually, he would stop at some point when I screamed, "Stop" ... maybe not instantly but almost always within fifty yards. My instinct was to scold him for bolting and doing something unsafe, but that would have been a mistake. I forced myself to praise him and thank him for stopping.

Walking tag point #4: Stand/Wait

The final skill we tackled was Stand/Wait. This skill was important because Doug needed to be able to wait with me at street corners and in the check-out line in the grocery store. Usually he would bounce, jiggle and shriek and I had to hold him in place—not pleasant. The Stand/Wait tag point is basically an extension of the Feet on Ground tag point discussed above, but with duration. I wanted Doug to stand for longer than a split second, preferably for at least 10-15 seconds and eventually, for three to four minutes in the grocery store checkout line. I set my next tag point as Stand/Wait Three Seconds.

Here is the analysis of the four criteria of the fourth tag point, Stand/Wait Three Seconds.:

1. **What I Want:** Doug waits at corners, crosswalks or in line at the grocery store.

2. **One Criterion**: YES. Doug has Feet on Ground for three seconds.

3. **Observable**: YES. I can see when Doug has both feet on the ground for up to three seconds. I could

also count how many instances of Stand/Wait Three Seconds occurred in a period of five or ten minutes.

4. **Five Words or Less:** YES. Stand/Wait Three Seconds is four words.

To teach Stand/Wait, I observed Doug's Feet on Ground behavior, and marked and reinforced it when he stopped for a bit longer than usual. I started with a very brief instance of behavior and shaped it to a longer duration. By this point, Doug had learned to accept verbal praise and to respond to verbal cues, so I was able to use more words while working with him. To keep track of how long he was standing still, I counted out loud, "one, two, three," and marked and reinforced him if he could stand still until he made it to three. He got big treats and lots of praise if he could do it. Then, we made it a game: I challenged him to stand still while I counted to four, five and so on. I lavished praise and rewards on him for standing still for longer periods of time. If he couldn't do it, I said, "Well, next time you'll be able to do it." We came up with counting games to keep him standing still: alternate counting (parent says "one", child says or signs "two"; parent says "three," child says or signs "four," and so on); counting with rhymes ("one, two, buckle my shoe)"; or reciting poems and lyrics from songs. The possibilities here are limited only by the imagination. I had fun with my child, kept him engaged with words and numbers, and most importantly, kept him standing still until it was time to cross the street or pay the store clerk. I often used this at the bank, where the tellers were amused by all the counting, rhymes, and touch-your-nose games we played. It worked. Now my son can wait in the bank line and at the teller's window, and everybody there enjoys seeing him. If I don't bring him they ask, "Where is your son today?"

While we were doing these games, I specifically praised

Doug for Good Waiting. I wanted him to learn that the cue "Wait" means that he would stand still (and play number or word games) until I indicated that it was time to walk. The cue signal that I used for "Wait" was the sign for "Wait" plus the word "Wait."

When Doug could walk in a straight line, stay beside me, and stop and wait at the street corner or the store, our family life changed for the better. We were able to go out, take walks in the park, and get exercise. I could run to the store for groceries whenever I needed to, and my son had many more opportunities to participate with the family in the activities of daily life. Finally, walking is not only healthy for a child, but it is calming too. Generally at the half-mile point in our walks, I noticed that Doug became calmer. Frequent walks are now part of our family routine, with the result that we are all healthier and happier for getting out, getting some fresh air, and clearing our minds.

One final comment. While I was teaching my child these walking behaviors, I encountered various little problems. One problem I ran into early on while teaching Doug to walk in a straight line was that he was walking nicely in a straight line, but he was going agonizingly slowly. He would take a few dragging steps in the same direction, then dither and dally. After thinking through the problem, I set a temporary tag point of Bounces, Jumps, or Hops in Same Direction. I marked and reinforced every instance of bouncing, jumping, springing or hopping in the same direction during our walks, with dramatic results! Within a few weeks, Doug was running for 50-yard stretches and we were finally moving. From there on, it was easy to teach Walk Beside Me and the other necessary walking behaviors.

Another little problem was that my son would often dart into front yards and hit the branches of a shrub or tree. Why, I have no idea. To deal with this, I thought through the problem and decided to mark and increase reinforcement for Walk Beside Me. I told him, "The rule is we can't go into front yards; you must walk beside me." I increased reinforcement for Walk Beside Me and guided him back to the sidewalk if he roamed into a yard and whacked a bush. Whether he understood the reason for the rule I can't say, but he learned to stay with me and not roam into front yards. With this situation, I felt it was important to teach the concept of a rule, and that there are things that we just cannot do.

So, whenever we ran into some little problem, I thought about the behavior I wanted to see in my child, I identified the behavior in terms of a single criterion, then I marked and reinforced that behavior every time it occurred.

Chapter 4

Going into the Community

Car Trips

Some children with autism enjoy car trips and have no problem, but others may need teaching or support to make it through a car trip. Good car behavior is essential because parents need to be able to concentrate on traffic and not have to deal with a screaming, agitated child in the back seat. Before we could work on good car behavior, I had to get Doug into the car, and that also took some effort and planning.

After using the Walk Beside Me tag point to get to the car safely, Doug had to get into the car, and that sometimes took a while. For him, getting into the car was a change in the environment (from outside to inside, from open space to enclosed space), and it was a sensory challenge. I dealt with this by having a favored treat (reinforcer) ready. I said, “Look. I have a lollipop for you. As soon as you are in the car seat with your seat belt fastened, you can have it.” As soon as he was in the car seat with the belt fastened, I praised him and handed over the lollipop. I used this type of approach sparingly, since it can lead to a difficult situation if the child does not comply. In most cases it is better to mark and reinforce after the behavior occurs than to offer the reward before the behavior happens.

Some children might not like seat belts and protest. It is the law in most states that children wear seat belts. So when my child protested, there was no negotiation. I told him, “You must wear a seat belt. It is the law,” and ignored any protests. Even though my child has low verbal skills, and probably didn’t fully understand my words, he understood the tone of voice and recognized that it was futile to protest. This was a skill that Doug developed over time, although it required my insistence and persistence. Over time, he has become more and more able to understand and follow my directions.

My child would often bounce and flail in the car, so I had to come up with a way to get him calm and quiet. I realized that he already had some good skills: the Quiet Voice and Good Walking behaviors discussed in previous chapters. He could get to the car safely and climb into the car seat, but he could not sit calmly. I decided to teach him Nice Sitting, and defined this as a combination of two skills: Hands Still and Feet Still. So, the behaviors I marked and reinforced were all instances of Hands Still and Feet Still.

Analysis of the tag point Hands Still:

1. **What I Want**: Doug sits calmly in the car without unnecessary hand movement.

2. **One Criterion**: YES. Doug's hands are still.
3. **Observable**: YES. I can see when Doug's hands are still. I could also count how many instances of Hands Still occurred in a period of five or ten minutes.
4. **Five Words or Less**: YES. Hands Still is two words.

Analysis of the tag point Feet Still:

1. **What I Want**: Doug sits calmly in the car without unnecessary foot movement.
2. **One Criterion**: YES. Doug's feet are still.
3. **Observable**: YES. I can see when Doug's feet are still. I could also count how many instances of Feet Still occurred in a period of five or ten minutes.
4. **Five Words or Less**: YES. Feet Still is two words.

The best way for us to teach this was to start with short car trips, with one person driving and another person marking and reinforcing the child for Quiet Mouth and other desired behaviors. (It's not even necessary to drive the car; it can be parked in the driveway.) To extend the length of time that my son could do Quiet Mouth, I used the same Stand/Wait procedure of counting: count to three, then mark and reinforce. Again, while we don't want our children to shriek and scream, we do want them to vocalize appropriately, so I marked and reinforced every instance of Good Sound/Word. We don't want the child thrashing about in the car, so I marked and reinforced Nice Sitting behaviors: Hands Still and Feet Still. At first, I was able to mark only one Hand Still or one Foot Still, but was eventually able to mark and reinforce when both hands or both feet were still.

Finally, it helped to have a basket of toys or activities that was reserved specifically for the car. As Doug learned to perform Quiet Mouth and Hands/Feet Still for longer periods, I handed the toys to him one at a time. We rotated the toys periodically so they remained fresh and interesting. He also enjoyed picture pages of the places we were going to visit (we slipped the picture page into a plastic sleeve so they lasted longer). These can be pleasing for a child because he knows where he is going, plus you can point to the pictures and name the people, places and objects he will see. We had great success with picture pages, not only of the places we were going to, but also picture pages with favorite objects, grocery store items, or animals. Picture pages can be printed and clipped into a folder, or digital and loaded onto a device.

Once I reach my destination, there is the challenge of getting my child out of the car and walking safely through the parking lot to the building or park. To get Doug out of the car, which is again a potential sensory issue because it is another change in the environment, I had a nice treat ready and was able to use the tag point Feet on Ground. As soon as Doug was out and had Feet on Ground, I marked, reinforced and gave him a lollipop.

To navigate from the car through the parking lot to the building or playground, we used the Walk Beside Me cue, and he would walk beside me to the final destination.

Combining the behaviors Doug had already learned for Quiet Mouth and Nice Walking with the behaviors of Nice Sitting allowed our entire family to get out more and enjoy life. After Doug mastered these skills, we were able to go more places on the spur of the moment. As always with autism, we had to monitor Doug's behavior and responses, and make adjustments as required by each situation.

The Grocery Store

To teach Doug to go to the grocery story, we used the three previously-taught tag points—Quiet Mouth, Walk Beside Me, and Stand/Wait—and taught a new tag point: Hands on Cart. My goal was to take Doug with me to the grocery store and have a nice time shopping for food for the family.

The grocery story is a challenging environment for kids with autism: bright lights, noise, tinny music, people milling about, water sprayers misting the vegetables, and my pet peeve, coupon dispensers with blinking red lights waving coupons right at eye level. Also, the child senses that the parent is somewhat distracted by having to shop for food. Under these adverse circumstances, the parent has to get the child through the grocery store, hopefully with no tantrums or bolting, and with something for the family to eat.

Good grocery store behavior has to be specifically taught. Before I started, I spoke with the manager of the store to explain that I was going to be teaching my child with autism to behave in the store, and I asked for their understanding. The people in my local grocery store were wonderfully supportive, friendly and helpful. I started this teaching by making multiple short trips where we purchased only a few items. I planned our purchases in advance and wrote up the list in the order that that we would walk through the store. Backtracking in the grocery store can be tough for a kid with autism, so we worked on that skill later.

Using the Walk Beside Me skill, I walked with Doug into the grocery store. The next step was to teach Hands on Cart. I asked Doug to help push the cart, then marked and reinforced him for Hands on Cart. (If a child is still small enough to sit in the cart, teach Hands on Cart anyway; it is a useful skill to build for the future.) When we walked through the produce aisle and had to stop the cart to pick out apples, I marked and reinforced my son for Stand/Wait. Eventually I could ask Doug to help put the apples in the bag and put the bag in the cart. I marked and reinforced any and all cooperative behaviors. When we set off for the next aisle, I marked and reinforced him for both good Walk Beside Me behavior and more Hands on Cart behavior.

Analysis of the tag point Hands on Cart:

1. **What I Want**: Doug keeps his hands on the cart (and eventually helps push the cart through the store).
2. **One Criterion**: YES. Tag point is Hands on Cart.
3. **Observable:** YES. I can see when Doug has both hands on the cart. I could also count how many instances of Hands on Cart occurred in a period of five or ten minutes.
4. **Five Words or Less**: YES. Hands on Cart is three words.

I kept marking and reinforcing all the good behaviors Doug was exhibiting. If he had Quiet Mouth throughout the trip, he could pick out a special treat in his favorite aisle. After more practice, we built these short trips into the normal routine that most parents have with their children at the grocery store. We could talk about the food items, count out the apples and oranges as we put them in the bag, discuss whether the bag was heavy or light, and so forth.

We applied this same skillset to stores where you shop with a shopping basket. In this case, the skill was Hand on Basket. I had my son hold one handle of the basket, while I held the other handle. We continued marking and reinforcing Walk With Me behavior and he stayed right with me.

Doug has excellent store behavior now, and one of his favorite expeditions is to a local market with wonderful bread rolls. We use a trip to the market as a reinforcer for other good behaviors, which is a useful thing. Also, the people in the store know him, like him and greet him warmly. I am always surprised that for so many people, our son is the first child with autism they have ever seen. It shows that many children with autism are isolated from their communities, and that the community is ignorant about the prevalence and problems of autism.

Other Types of Stores

In stores where you do not use a cart or basket to shop, we focused intensively on the Walk Beside Me tag point described above. I started with short trips and marked and reinforced Walk Beside Me until I was confident that Doug would stay with me and not bolt down those long, tempting aisles.

Going to the Park and Playground

To take Doug to the park and playground, we used all the tag points mentioned above for getting him into the car, sitting nicely in the car, getting out of the car, and walking to the park area or playground.

For walking through the park, I used the Walk Beside Me cue to keep Doug with me. These walks were also a great time to mark and reinforce any other nice behaviors, such as climbing over a log or throwing stones in a creek.

When I head for the playground, we face a loud, busy environment. The playground can be a very high-stress place for a child with autism—lots of loud noises, shouting, running kids, and strange scary-looking contraptions. Armed with a box clicker and treats, I was able to mark and reinforce every single "good" muscle movement that Doug made, no matter how inconsequential it appeared. Looks at slide, mark! Takes a step, mark! Looks at bird, mark! Turns (even partially) toward me, mark! Puts foot on a step, mark! Reaches for a bar, mark! After a while, Doug calmed down because he was being reinforced for whatever he was doing, and no one was pushing him to do things that were uncomfortable. He learned that putting his feet on the first step of the ladder resulted in lots of reinforcement, and that going up another step resulted in more treats and praise. This shaping process was a way to calm my child and encourage him to explore the environment, and it was a great way for me to do creative marking and reinforcing (marking unexpected but "good" or "cute" behaviors).

Waiting in the Doctor's Office

Taking a child with autism to the doctor is often a difficult, stressful experience for parents, even if that child is not the one who is sick. Parents may wish to call ahead and ask to have a room ready when they walk in so they don't have a long wait in the public waiting area. People with disabilities are entitled to accommodations, so especially when dealing with a doctor or dentist, don't hesitate to ask for help. We learned to ask the office staff to phone in any prescription for the pharmacy; that way it was ready for us and we eliminated a second waiting period at the pharmacy with a sick child.

To get to the car, through the car trip and into the doctor's office, we used the Walk Beside Me, Nice Sitting and Nice Voice behaviors described above. We also brought a special Waiting Room Toy Kit. For years I had a small suitcase packed with toys and activities for Doug that he could only do in the waiting room.

It was always in the closet at home and was used only for this one purpose. He actually became cheerful when he saw me pull it out. I handed the activities to him one at a time and marked and reinforced him for doing them. Initially, the toy kit lasted only a short time in keeping Doug engaged, but as he learned and grew he was able to stick with the activities for longer periods. Naturally, other children in the family can play with those items too. There is a lot of juggling for any autism mom in the doctor's office with a sick child with autism, one who is healthy, perhaps an infant, or a different combination of who is sick and who is healthy. If there is a plan of action in place and all the children know that they will have toys, activities and treats, this difficult task can go more smoothly. With the proliferation of devices and game applications available now, there are many more options for keeping a child occupied in the waiting room.

The Waiting Room Toy Kit, plus lots of marking and reinforcing for Quiet Mouth, helped Doug learn to behave nicely in waiting rooms. By the time he was a teenager, he could wait calmly in the orthodontist's waiting room for up to forty-five minutes, with no toy kit and no treats, while our other child had his braces adjusted.

Chapter 5

Self-Stimulatory and Boisterous Behaviors

We worked on reducing self-stimulatory physical behaviors by marking and reinforcing the following tag points:

- Hands Still
- Arms Still
- Feet Still
- Head Still
- Sits on Chair

The goal was to reduce disruptive physical behaviors and increase appropriate play behaviors.

Children with autism can display lots of self-stimulatory behaviors. We never liked these and worked hard to reduce them. Reducing these behaviors and giving Doug replacement behaviors seemed to calm him and give him more enjoyment of life. To determine where to start, I found it helpful to do a five-minute observation of my child.

Dr. Martin Kozloff in his book *Educating Children with Learning and Behavior Problems* provides the following directions:

> For 5 minutes, *observe* the behavior of the child . . .. do not talk to him. Sit or stand across the room from where he is and watch the *movements* he is making. Watch the way he moves his hands and eyes. What does he touch? What does he look at? Listen to the sounds that he makes. Listen well enough so that you could write them down. Watch his eyes when he makes sounds. Does he look at anyone else?

I sat down, as suggested above, and took notes on the specific physical movements Doug made. I watched to see if he was hopping, bouncing or running. I noted whether he was hopping on one foot or alternating. I observed whether he was waving his left arm, right arm or both arms. Was he silent or shrieking? Running back and forth or in circles? The notes gave me a very good idea of which parts of the body my child was moving in a self-stimulatory or repetitive way. I could then decide which physical movement to address first. Since Doug, like many children with autism, flapped his hands or waggled his fingers, I decided to work on Hands Still.

To teach Hands Still, I sat near my child in a room and waited for him to demonstrate a Hands Still moment. Even though it may seem that a child's hands are always moving, behavior is variable and what a child is doing will change. At some point, the child's hand will be still, or down at his side or in an acceptable position. As soon as I saw one hand still or in an acceptable position, I marked and reinforced that movement. If one hand was still and the other hand was moving, I marked and reinforced the one Still Hand. After I had been marking and reinforcing Doug for one Hand Still and I saw that he was getting the idea, I sat back to see if he could perform two Hands Still. I continued marking and reinforcing Hands Still. If he couldn't perform two Hands Still very often, I went back to marking and reinforcing him for just one Hand Still. Shaping towards Hands Still for several short (five to ten minute) sessions each day noticeably reduced the hand waving. I kept marking and reinforcing Hands Still as much as possible until it became a strong, reliable behavior. I found that it was also possible to set tag points such as Touch Toy, Touch Book, Touch Pencil, and to mark and reinforce him every time his hands were occupied with an appropriate behavior.

It may be helpful here to review the rules for tag points and how often to reinforce a desired behavior. The four criteria for a tag point are:

1. What I Want
2. One Criterion
3. Observable
4. Five Words or Less

In the following sections, the tag points are named, but not formally analyzed as frequently; criteria can be inferred from the descriptions. Regarding reinforcement, our metaphor is: when building a house you fasten every single board, window and door into place. Once the house is built, you stop fastening every piece in place and switch to maintenance (cleaning and repair).

When building a behavior, you mark and reinforce it every time you see it (continuous reinforcement schedule). Once the behavior is established, you switch to maintenance by marking and reinforcing every now and then (variable reinforcement). Be sure to reinforce any time the child does the behavior under difficult conditions (for example in a new place, in the presence of noise or distractions, etc.) or does the behavior particularly well or with great enthusiasm.

To reduce rocking, spinning and toe-walking, I considered the following tag points: Back on Chair, Back Straight, and Heel on Ground. To reduce rocking, which Doug occasionally did in a chair or the back seat of the car, I used the tag point Back on Chair. As soon as his back hit the back of the chair, I marked and reinforced. Usually this led to an extinction burst where the rocking accelerated but then tapered off. When Doug did free-style rocking—rocking while sitting on the floor or someplace with no chair—I marked and reinforced him for Back Straight when he was upright. Doug did a lot of spinning and occasional toe-walking in the early years, and the only way we had to deal with it was physically stopping him. If I could do it over, I would mark and reinforce Feet on Ground and Heel on Ground intensively. To reduce spinning, I would use the Feet on Ground tag point: wait and observe until both feet are motionless on the ground, then mark and reinforce that behavior. To reduce toe-walking, I would use the tag point Heel on Ground. Just as a reminder, I did not verbalize these tag points (at least not at first), I just waited for them to happen so that I could mark them. Adding the cue for the behavior with a word or a hand signal came only after Doug offered the behavior reliably.

Children with autism have a lot of energy and often expend it through boisterous behaviors. If a child has a lot of energy and engages in behaviors like climbing up bookcases and bouncing on the sofa, parents are advised to "redirect" the behavior and teach an alternative behavior that is more acceptable. Well, the devil is in the details. In the early years, Doug could not stand still for one second, could not sit still for one second, and had no interest in toys, crayons or blocks. I didn't know how to build up nice sitting and play behaviors from chaos, and would try seating him at the play table with toys to no avail. I have thought about this for a long time, and if I could do it over, I have some ideas about how I would shape those behaviors now.

I would set up two places in the home for activities: a play table with toys and craft items, and an active area where the child can safely engage in jumping and bouncing activities. My active area would have a small trampoline and large foam blocks and mats that stack to safely fill in as a climbing structure. I would make these two areas appealing to a child by marking and reinforcing whenever he is near one of them. Tag points could be: Looks at Play Table, Walks Toward Play Table, Sits at Play Table, Looks at Active Area, Goes to Active Area, Plays in Active Area. I would shape the desired behavior by gradually raising the criteria through these tag points that move successively toward the final goal, staying with one tag point a few times and only moving to the next one when the child begins to offer the next behavior. For example, if I was marking and reinforcing Looks at Play Table and I started to notice that the child is starting to take some steps toward the play table, only then would I raise the criteria and begin marking and reinforcing Walks Toward Play Table. I would be sure that the next part of the behavior is already starting to happen on its own, before I start expecting it. If I find that my rate of reinforcement is dropping (that is I am tagging less frequently), then I would go back to an easier tag point so that my child maintains interest and does not become frustrated.

I would also do double duty: while I am marking and

reinforcing the child for the tag points designed to reduce self-stimulatory behaviors (Hands Still, etc.), I would place the treats for the child in one of these two activity areas. This will accustom the child to going to those two spots. Every once in a while, I would place a special treat in the play areas and let the child find it. These actions will bring home to the child the message that the play table and the active area are fun places to be.

In the active area, I would mark and reinforce Climbs on Foam Blocks or Jumps on Trampoline. If the child veers off to the bookcases to climb, or to the sofa to bounce, I would simply guide him away. I would also say, "The rule is, we only climb on the blocks," or "The rule is, we only bounce on the trampoline." Whether my son understood these spoken rules, I was never sure, but I felt I had to tell him what he could and could not do. We had terrible problems with my son doing full-length body drops on the sofa, but solved that problem in one day when we set up a trampoline. I feel that it is important for a child with autism to understand limits and that destruction of property in the house is unacceptable. But it is also important for that child to have acceptable ways to expend energy. Having a child play in the active play area, plus going for walks, can use up some of that energy.

Our children engage in other behaviors such as water play, coloring or fabric and paper-ripping, which may or may not be acceptable depending on the situation. The problems arise when the behaviors result in messes or damage. Children with autism often love water play, and this is fine provided they don't flood the sink. It is possible to teach a child to play with water appropriately by setting aside one particular sink (reduce the water flow to the faucet in that sink), setting out water toys and teaching him to clean up any water spills. Tag points for teaching these behaviors could be Requests Water Play, Uses Water Toys, and Wipes Up Spills. I would mark and reinforce the child for all appropriate water play actions. If some water spills, I hand him a paper towel and have him wipe up the spill; then mark him for cleaning up. I believe that a child with autism needs to get the idea that they have to clean up their messes just like everybody else. My son became very good at spotting messes, and would charge into the kitchen for a paper towel to clean them up. It was hilarious to see the serious, determined look on his face. He knew what to do and he was proud of himself.

It is possible to use water play as a reinforcer for other activities by saying, "When we get back from our walk, you can play with water," or, "After you eat lunch, you can play with water." To make it easier to leave the activity, I would tell Doug before water play begins, "When water play is over, you will get a lollipop." It can also be helpful to set a timer for the amount of playtime that is appropriate. When the timer went off and water play was over, I often gave my child a treat and praised him for playing nicely. All desired activities have to end, so this helped my son learn that the end of an activity had its positive aspects.

Coloring and painting are fine activities for our kids, provided they don't do it on the walls or furniture. Like water play, coloring is an activity that I limit to one or two areas in the house. I would put some coloring materials on the play table that the child has been getting used to, and mark and reinforce him for approaching and sitting at the play table.

I plan to spend some time on reinforcing the child for sitting at the table; this is an important behavior and I want it to be a strong one. When I started working with my son years ago, the advice was to sit at a table and start working on a series of exercises to teach basic skills. The only problem was, his behavior was so wild and chaotic that there was no way to get him to the chair, let alone sit on it. I struggled with that issue for a long time, and eventually got him to sit on the chair, but it was a slow, painful process. Had TAGteach been available to me at that time, the task would have been easier and probably would have gone more quickly. If I had to do it over, I would approach it in the way I describe below.

I would identify the goal as having the child sit in the chair for a short time, then for increasingly longer periods. My thoughts are: first, I would set the chair out so the child can quickly and easily sit in it and get up. Next, I would mark and reinforce the following tag points: Looks at Chair, Walks To/Near Chair, Sits on Chair. This is another example of shaping, where each successive tag point moves the child closer to the goal. I would continue reinforcing these tag points until the child learns that sitting on the chair is nice because he gets attention and praise. Once I get the child to sit on the chair, I would work on lengthening the time in the same way as was discussed in teaching waiting at the store.

Now, the behavior to mark and reinforce would be Stay on Chair. I might challenge the child to stay on the chair while I count to three, four, five and so on. I would praise and reward lavishly for sitting still for longer periods of time. If the child cannot do it, I just say "Well, next time you'll be able to do it." Next time, I would try again to get the child to sit for a short period. Counting games and rhymes are a great way to hold the child's interest as long as possible, and while I am doing this, I would casually hand him an item from the play table. The goal is for the child's attention to transition to the toys and crayons on the table. Tag points for the play table would be similar to those for water play: Goes to Play Table, Sits on Chair, Requests Coloring, Colors on Paper, Requests Toy, Touches Toy, Plays With Toy, Touches Book. This is an opportunity to use my special knowledge of what my child likes to do. I mark and reinforce all nice actions during coloring time and play time. If Doug wandered off with a crayon and headed for a wall, I gently guided him back to the play table, and said, "The rule is, we only color at the table."

Paper and fabric-ripping are also things our children may like to do, and both are undesirable, destructive behaviors. My son had the bad habit of poking his fingers into sofa cushions until he made a little hole, then ripping the fabric and pulling out the stuffing. The general recommendation for these kinds of problems is to redirect destructive activity to something related, but acceptable. A potential, alternate activity to ripping could be pulling stickers off a roll and sticking them onto paper, or tearing off and replacing pieces of Velcro from cardboard or foam trays. If the child starts to rip anything else, I might say, "The rule is, rip Velcro. Let's go over to the table and you can play with stickers and Velcro." I would gently guide the child to the play table and mark and reinforce the child for Pulls off Stickers, Pulls Velcro, Stickers on Paper Plate, Velcro on Cardboard. There are lots of imaginative ways to set this up as a counting or art activity: first piece of cardboard has one Velcro strip, second piece has two strips, and so forth, or make designs such as squares, rectangles and triangles from Velcro strips.

Another acceptable substitute activity could be playing with picture magnets; there are many nice magnetic toys available that give the sensation of ripping something off of a surface. Initially, I would mark and reinforce the child for peeling off stickers, magnets and Velcro at the play table as much as he likes, then start to reduce the number of stickers available and encourage him to do other activities, perhaps play-dough, stacking cups, or links. One approach to expand the range of activities could be to have the child touch or briefly play with another toy in order to "earn" the next sticker or piece of Velcro (tag point would be Touch Toy). As soon as the child touches the toy, I would mark and reinforce by giving him the next sticker or piece of Velcro. Over time, I could increase the number of toys to touch and the length of time he is occupied with a toy before giving him a sticker or Velcro. I would mark and reinforce the child for doing anything other than stickers and Velcro; additional tag points could be: Touches Other Toy, Plays With Other Toy, Touches Paint Brush, etc.

Some more thoughts: A child may not want to leave the play table or active area. If so, that is wonderful! If he asks for more time, I would say "Yes, you can play a bit longer, but first I want you to do something." Then I would set a short, easy task for the child. In the beginning, it would be a task that he can do without leaving the play table: something as simple as touching an object. Naturally, I would mark and reinforce the child for doing the task. This procedure will start to teach the child that he has to work to "earn" his play privileges. Over time, the tasks could become more like real-life tasks (putting a pencil in the pencil tray, setting a book or toy on a shelf, carrying a dish to the kitchen), and increase the number of tasks. I want Doug to be able to transition calmly from play to work and back again, and know that this is a normal routine. As always with autism, it's important to observe the child and make adjustments according to each situation and the child's needs.

Chapter 6

Social Skills

Eye Contact

Many parents want our children with autism to look at us and not contort their faces. As autism parents, we frequently see children with a variety of facial behaviors. Whenever I see these, I try to think about how one could mark and reinforce more appropriate expressions. My thoughts about decreasing unusual eye/facial behaviors and increasing eye contact are to work on what I call Nice Looking, which can be shaped using the following tag points:

- Head Up
- Head Facing Forward
- Eyes on Speaker's Face

Remember always to assess each tag point according to the four tag point criteria:

1. What I Want
2. One Criterion
3. Observable
4. Five Words or Less

Children with autism often have unusual eye behaviors. My son often squints and flutters his eyelashes. Sometimes children may stare fixedly at some object or roll their eyes around wildly, and they often avoid eye contact. Children may also make unusual grimaces or other facial movements. Generally, we would like to decrease odd eye behaviors and increase nice eye behaviors. I would start by observing the child's eye movements for a while and make notes of the specific eye movements he makes. Next, I would determine which eye behaviors I would like to see, set up tag points that describe these specific eye movements, then mark and reinforce those movements when they occur. Since many variations in eye movements are possible, I will share my thoughts about a few common situations.

If the child stares fixedly at a particular object, I would observe this behavior and see how long he maintains that gaze and measure the time with a stopwatch. I would start with the tag point Eyes Look at Another Object. I would watch the child's eyes, and as soon as he moves his gaze to another object, mark and reinforce. I keep this up until the child's fixed gazing behavior is lessened. It may be useful to set out interesting objects and tag the child for looking at a variety of objects, then set out objects in a row and have the child look at each object in turn. The tag point for this would be Looks at Object. When the child can look at a number of objects in sequence, I could shift to looking at pictures in sequence and teach scanning. This would be a valuable precursor skill for reading. I would work on these tag points specifically during several short sessions (8-10 minutes) per day, or just keep an eye out for the behaviors during the course of the day and mark and reinforce whenever I spot it. Each family has different time and schedule commitments. We made progress with both approaches.

Next, I would like my child to look at me. Eye contact is highly prized in Western cultures because we associate it with honesty and attentiveness, so it is important to teach. Again, I would observe the child's eye contact behavior and assess how he avoids eye contact. Does he keep his eyes to the side, hold his head to the side, lower his head or some combination of these behaviors? The initial tag point may be Head Up or Head Faces Forward. With these tag points, the child initially may only be able to partially keep his head up or face forward; I would mark and reinforce a partial response as part of the shaping process. The final tag point I would work on is Eyes on Speaker's Face. I would mark and reinforce every glance where the child's gaze rests, even if very fleetingly, on my face or the face of another speaker in the room. I would start introducing the child's name as a cue for looking at me. When the child's gaze rests on my face I would say, "Douglas", then mark and reinforce. Then I would keep combining the child's name with his gaze and start saying his name earlier until I am saying it before he looks at me. If I say "Douglas" and he does not look at me, I then go back to combining name with gaze, but keep trying. When I can reliably say my child's name and he looks at me, I can congratulate myself on having taught a valuable social and academic behavior.

Facial Behaviors

To increase nice facial behaviors, I would start by studying the child's facial movements for a while and observe what he does with cheeks, mouth and tongue. Often young children with autism will stick out their tongues, or stretch their cheeks or mouths in odd contortions. In the early years, my son always had his tongue lolling out of his mouth. We fought the "Battle of the Tongue" for years. It would go away for a long time and then re-emerge. If I could do it over, I would set the tag point of Tongue In, and mark and reinforce that behavior relentlessly. I have seen children push out their cheeks constantly with their tongue; in this case, I would try the tag point Cheeks Flat. I would mark and reinforce these desired movements every time I see them and praise the child when he has a pleasant face with no grimaces. This is a perfect time to tell the child how beautiful or handsome he is. Also, I am on the lookout for really nice faces; so I can mark and reinforce the child for Smiles, Happy Face, or any kind of facial appearance that I feel is pleasant and appropriate.

Social Interaction

Once a child is better able to make eye contact, it may be a good time to work on improving interaction skills. If the child has learned imitation skills, I might want to have him imitate me when he looks at me. I could clap my hands or touch my nose and see if he does the same. The tag point would be Imitates Action, and I would tag and treat if he imitates my gesture. If he doesn't imitate, I just wait and try, try again. The next step could be to teach him to imitate a variety of gestures or to have him repeat a word, if he is verbal. The tag point would be Repeats Word(s). I would start off with "Hi" and mark and reinforce my child if he says "Hi" back to me. Then I would keep working on other words: point to other objects in the room, name them and try to get the child to say the name. Here is a potential sequence: child gives eye contact, I mark and reinforce eye contact, I point to a chair and say, "Chair." If the child repeats "chair" then I mark and reinforce; if the child does not repeat the word, I would try again later or lower my expectations and make it easier for the child to succeed.

Many children with autism have echolalia, where the problem itself is repeating the words heard, so this would not be the approach to use with them. For decreasing echolalia, the tag point could be Says Something Different. I would mark and reinforce all instances where the child does not repeat what I say but makes a different response, even if it is only a sneeze or grunt. Another tag point might be Quiet Mouth (just to get some peace and quiet).

Sometimes kids with autism have verbal skills, but they can't move a conversation forward beyond the first or second response. They get stuck on a concept, can't express what they are thinking and may become frustrated and angry. One way to encourage longer conversations could be to reinforce additional responses. At first, I would mark and reinforce one-response or two-response exchanges, until the child is comfortable with those, then see if it is possible to move up to three-response exchanges. This could be an additional way to build a behavior chain of comment/ response, comment/response, keeping in mind that for many children the hard part is first, "manufacturing" the response and second, building up the endurance to keep the response chain going. My profoundly nonverbal son can now participate with us in verbal exchanges with fifteen or more responses. These are not actually "verbal," in that they are scripted, repetitive conversations, but the fact that we are even having this kind of interaction is amazing to us. And my son enjoys them very much. As always, observe and monitor the child and make adjustments according to each unique situation and the child's reactions.

Chapter 7

Going to Sleep

Sleep that knits up the ravelled
sleave of care
The death of each day's life, sore
labour's bath
Balm of hurt minds, great nature's
second course,
Chief nourisher in life's feast.

William Shakespeare, "Macbeth"

Of all the difficult, vexing behaviors of children with autism, the most grievous problem is not sleeping. Our children with autism often cannot fall asleep or stay asleep, leaving the parents worn out, exhausted and short-tempered. Continuous lack of sleep causes huge problems for parents at their jobs, and for siblings who are continually being awakened by shrieking or commotion. It extends the agony of autism throughout the night. It is exhausting and depressing beyond description.

Many parents find themselves lying down with their child for hours to get him to sleep, bringing the child into their own bed, taking the child to another bed or room in the house, and then having to deal with the problem all over again during the inevitable night-time wake-ups. Struggling with sleep problems for four to eight hours a night is not unusual. We dealt with those problems for years, and I found TAGteach to offer useful solutions. TAGteach was not around when Doug was small, and it would have made our lives so much easier at bedtime and during middle-of-the-night wake-ups. When I learned about TAGteach, I was able to teach Doug to lie still, be quiet, and go to sleep.

In tackling sleeping problems, we found the following steps helpful: (1) set a consistent wake-up time early in the morning and a consistent bedtime in the evening, (2) avoid large meals or snacks late in the evening, and (3) reinforce the tag points Quiet Mouth, Hands Still, Feet Still, Head on Pillow, Yawns and Exhales.

To start, we implemented Step 1: set consistent wake-up and bedtimes. We got Doug up, dressed and moving every day by 7:00 a.m. at the latest, or even 6:30 or 6:00. We did not let him sleep late, take naps or doze off in the car. We did whatever it took to keep him awake and moving for the entire day, and enacted all kinds of antics to keep him from falling asleep in the car or on the sofa during the day. A consistent bedtime is also very important.

Ironically, we learned that an earlier bedtime worked better for Doug than a later one. We initially thought that if he went to bed later, he would be more tired. Wrong. We finally figured out that a later bedtime meant he was more tired, but also more wound up, agitated and cranky. For us, an earlier bedtime works better.

We then implemented Step 2: make sure Doug had no big meals or heavy snacks in the evening, because this might give him an energy boost.

The big job was implementing Step 3, reinforcing the tag points Quiet Mouth, Hands Still, Feet Still, Head On Pillow, Yawns and Exhales. In the evening, we went through the usual family bedtime routine. Then I gently put Doug to bed, explained that it was time to be quiet, stay in bed, and go to sleep. Doug was about nine or ten at this point, and whether he was able to understand everything, I don't know. As a parent, I felt I should explain my expectations.

I turned off all the lights in the room and hallway, and went out of the room. From that point on, I reinforced the following tag points—Quiet Mouth, Hands Still, Feet Still, Head on Pillow, Yawns and Exhales. There are two ways to reinforce these desired behaviors: from outside the room or from inside the room. In the beginning, I always reinforced from outside the room, but I recently found that I could also reinforce from inside the room. For either approach, I found the following materials helpful:

- comfortable, loose clothing
- a flashlight (it is better to use a flashlight at night for marking the behavior rather than a clicker, because the flashlight is silent and will not disrupt other family members)
- a comfortable, padded high stool to sit on (I found it works better to sit on a high stool than a chair, because it's easier and less tiring to jump up constantly from a stool than a chair)

From Outside the Room: I sat outside the bedroom (on the stool) with the bedroom door slightly ajar so I could observe Doug, then waited until I could mark and reinforce any of the following tag points: Quiet Mouth, Hands Still, Feet Still or Anything Still. Behavior is variable, so a child who is shrieking and bouncing around will, at some point for a split second, stop shrieking or stop moving some part of his body. When Doug had a split second of Quiet Mouth or Still Body Part, I flashed the light, went in and gave him a gentle pat on the shoulder or arm. I did not talk to him or explain, and left immediately. Then, I sat outside and waited for the next instance of Quiet Mouth, Still Body Part, Head On Pillow or Yawns. It took a long time, but eventually he fell asleep.

To review, here is the procedure I used:

- I flashed the light and went in the room and patted his arm every single time he was quiet or still.

- I did not go in if he was screaming or jumping, no matter how loud and anguished he sounded.

- If he bolted from the room, I took him by the hand and gently lead him back to the bed. Then, I returned to my post outside the room and waited for him to do any one of the tag points listed above; I kept flashing the light and rewarding him with my presence and attention. I kept this up until he calmed down. Eventually he did calm down, get into bed, and lie still.

- After time went by and he appeared to be drifting off to sleep, I decided it might be better to continue to go into the room, but not pat him—I didn't want to wake him—but instead I leaned quietly over the bed or patted the pillow.

Naturally at the beginning, there was a powerful extinction burst of loud, disruptive behavior, and I simply had to outlast it.

This process took a long time for us: several hours per night the first few weeks, to get the new, desired behaviors going, then several months to teach them so my child could keep them up. But they worked. For a long time, Doug went to sleep nicely.

But time passed, I got lazy and failed to do the "maintenance" work to keep this behavior in good shape. Recently I had to patch it up again, since it had descended into a shambles. Doug was staying in bed, but had developed a terrible repertoire of noises, including an incredibly annoying burbling slurp that drove me wild; plus, he bolted out of the room constantly. The noise was awful: shriek, yowl, slurp/slurp/slurp, pounding footsteps and slamming doors. When I restarted the process, I decided to take notes: I kept track of what time Doug went to bed and what time he fell asleep. I also counted how many times I flashed the light and went into the room to pat him on the shoulder (to mark and reinforce the desired behaviors of Quiet Mouth and Still Body Part). Here is the raw data from my notes from the first few days:

Day	Time Started	Time Finished	Total Time	No. of Flashes
Thursday	10:25 p.m.	2:00 a.m.	3 hrs. 35 min.	536
Friday	9:47 p.m.	11:30 p.m.	1 hr. 43 min.	241
Saturday	10:17 p.m.	11:25 p.m.	1 hr. 8 min.	158
Sunday	10:27 p.m.	12:45 a.m.	2 hrs. 18 min.	335
Monday	10:10 p.m.	12:22 a.m.	2 hrs. 12 min.	295
Tuesday	10:15 p.m.	11:34 p.m.	1 hr. 19 min.	216

The first night, Thursday, it took a long, long time. Friday and Saturday nights were shorter, and then, extinction burst! Sunday and Monday took a long time again. On Tuesday, the time decreased. My notes showed some progress, but also that it was still taking a long time to get him to sleep. I kept up the routine of sitting outside the room, but fatigue and impatience drove me to try another approach, and I experimented with working from inside the room. I had never tried this because I thought it would not work; if I was already in the room, how could my presence be reinforcing for my child? When I tried working from inside the room, I found that things moved faster. I was better able to decrease the amount of time he was awake and increase the amount of time he was asleep. He also stopped making noises and stopped bolting out of the room.

From Inside the Room: I tried this one evening when I was simply could not face sitting outside on the stool. I was tired. My legs ached. So I plopped into a chair next to the bed. I sat in the chair and flashed the light and patted my son's arm every time he was quiet or still. I faced away from him if he was making noise or moving, but faced him to pat his arm when he was quiet or still. This approach, of sitting next to the bed, unexpectedly turned out to be more efficient for us. By chance, the chair I plopped into was a desk chair that swiveled. This made it easy to swivel toward him when he was quiet or still, and to swivel away when he started to shriek, bounce, or worst of all, slurp. Since I was sitting right next to him, I could reinforce Quiet Mouth and Arms/Legs Still, Head on Pillow or Yawns continuously; I fell into a steady routine of flash/pat, flash/pat, flash/pat. This intensive stream of reinforcement calmed him down more quickly and he fell asleep in less time than it took when I stayed outside the door. It worked! I was astonished, but pleased with the outcome.

Throughout this sleep-training project I made mistakes. In the beginning, when I was outside the room, I wasn't able to reinforce heavily enough. When building a behavior, it is important to do continuous reinforcement, and my reinforcement was not continuous enough. His vocal stimming was non-stop, so progress was slow until I sat next to him and figured out how to mark and reinforce each microsecond of Quiet Mouth between the slurps. I could only reinforce at such a heavy rate while sitting right next to him. Also, I learned that when he was quiet, I had to keep marking and reinforcing through the entire quiet moment. In fact, doing intensive flash/patting was the only way to keep the Quiet Mouth going. With time, he had longer and longer periods of quiet.

The next mistake was keeping this high-intensity reinforcement going on too long. After a behavior has been built, it is time to change from a continuous reinforcement schedule to a variable reinforcement schedule (reinforce at different intervals). I realized at one point that there were longer periods of quiet between the slurps and bounces, so I tried to see if it would work to wait a bit longer before I flashed the light and patted his arm. To do this I would flash/pat, then wait one, two, or three seconds, to see if he could stay quiet for a longer time. He was able to stay quiet, so I continued to experiment and lengthen the time between the flash/pats and thus reduce and vary the rate of reinforcement.

Another mistake was marking a behavior too soon or too late. Sometimes, when I anticipated a micro-second of quiet between the slurps and flashed the light, he would suddenly do an extended slurp, so I inadvertently marked and reinforced an undesired behavior. Sometimes he would be quiet, and I failed to catch it promptly. Fortunately, TAGteach is very forgiving of such errors. Most of the time I marked and reinforced appropriately, and the desired behaviors grew stronger.

Despite the mistakes and frustration, after five months Doug was going to sleep nicely in a reasonable amount of time, and staying asleep through the night. Even if he was not asleep, he was now able to be quiet in his room and stay in bed, so we can sleep. As always with autism, there were touching and humorous moments. Doug really appreciated the help with falling asleep. He would carefully pick up the flashlight and hand it to me with an appealing look that said, "Here it is. Be sure to do this tonight." He even pushed the chair into position next to his bed and set the flashlight on the table right next to the chair, so everything would be ready to go. Also, while I was flashing and patting his arm, he would reach over to me and, very gently, pat my arm! Was he trying to reinforce me? I don't know. But it was very sweet. On the other hand, there were times when he would yank on my arm and yell, "Out!" It was an adventure with laughter and moments of frustration, but we ended up with a good outcome: for twenty to thirty minutes of work, we got six to seven hours of uninterrupted sleep—a real luxury for autism parents. I take pains to keep up the "maintenance" work by sitting next to his bed doing the flash/pat (mark/reinforce) routine. Often when I leave now, he is still awake, but he stays quiet, stays in bed and sleeps through the night.

By working from either outside or inside the room, I taught my child that being quiet and lying down in bed resulted in attention and affection from Mom, and that screaming and bouncing got him nothing. As a result, he learned to stay in bed, relax and fall asleep. In retrospect, I think sitting outside worked better when we had a lot of problems with him moving around his room. It was better to stay outside and then go in when he was not moving. Later, when he was staying in bed nicely, but was making annoying noises, it was better to work from inside the room. From inside I could reinforce Quiet Mouth intensively enough to change that behavior, plus, it was nice for him; I think that the process gave him a pleasant, gentle transition from waking to sleeping. Taking notes was very helpful. I created a Sleep Chart that allowed me to track the amount of time he was awake and asleep every night.

All of this was hard work, but that is life with autism. At least, I was sitting down, which was more restful than fuming and futilely trying to cajole my child to be quiet, and I had a strategy, which is much, much better than feeling helpless, distraught, and angry. It is important to remember that sleep problems are typical of children with autism, and should not be taken personally. Addressing them is a straightforward case of reinforcing good behaviors and ignoring bad behaviors. When I realized that I was dealing with a training problem, and that I had the ability to change it, I felt confident and competent. This confidence rubs off on Doug and helps him become more calm and quiet.

This is the hard part of autism: you can change even the most difficult behaviors, but it takes a lot of time and hard work, and there is nobody to do the work—except Mom and Dad, who have to work, take care of the other children, pay the bills and manage the household, and who also need to sleep and eat despite being isolated, upset and exhausted.

Chapter 8

Life Skills

Dressing and Toileting

Dressing and toileting are skills that require a child to perform a series of physical movements in a specific order. This series of steps is referred to as a "behavior chain." In his excellent book, *Educating Children with Learning and Behavior Problems,* Dr. Kozloff (page 355) describes a behavior chain as:

1. Help the child to hook up or chain smaller or simpler movements into the right order, so that they make up a more complete task or chore.

2. Get his chore behavior under the control of natural signals.

Dressing and toileting are behavior chains that require combinations of fine and gross motor skills, so there are two points to discuss here: improving fine and gross motor skills, and teaching behavior chains. Let's start with fine and gross motor skills.

Autism families like to do as much as they can to help their children gain skills in these areas. By teaching my son good walking behaviors and getting out to parks and playgrounds, we were naturally improving his gross motor skills. By using other times of the day when we were already busy with our child, we were able to enhance his fine motor skills. Bath time is a great opportunity for working on fine motor skills.

Car trips are another time when a child can do some fine motor activities: the Car Toy Box can include lacing cards, links and toys with knobs, dials and buttons. There are excellent products on the market for teaching dressing skills, such as dressing dolls and dressing books with zippers, buttons, and laces; these items can be included in the Car Toy Box or the Waiting Room Toy Kit. Also, there are helpful and charming books, videos and DVDs that do an excellent job of demonstrating dressing skills for children and showing them how to determine what is the front and back of each clothing item. It is worthwhile to get some of these and have the child watch them.

Once Doug had the necessary fine motor strength and could grasp, pinch, push and pull small objects, we could work on the dressing procedure. Dressing is a complex *set* of behavior chains because there is a sequence of different steps for each item of clothing, and then a series of these sequences for putting on those clothing items. The sequence for clothing that we used was as follows: underwear, socks, pants, shirt, shoes, jacket, hat, gloves (naturally, this sequence can be modified). We started by modeling dressing behaviors. On the advice of a therapist, I first dressed my son by either sitting or standing behind him. By watching my hands pull on the clothes he could see what his hands should be doing. We went through each step of the behavior chain and he gradually learned them. At that time, I did not know about TAGteach, but if I had to do it over, I would use tag points for each step in the dressing process.

For putting on underwear, my son had to learn to do the following physical movements in a chain: Hands Grasp Sides of Underpants, Bend Down, Lean Against Bed (optional), One Foot in Hole, Next Foot in Hole, Pull Pants Up. I had to insert the extra step of Lean Against Bed because my son did not have the balance to stand on one foot while placing the other foot in the hole of the underpants. The sequence for socks was Hands Grasp Sides of Sock, Sock On Toes, Finger in Heel of Sock, Pull Sock Up; repeat for other foot.

Putting on shirts properly with the label in back is another skill we had to teach. The first tag point that we used was Front of Shirt on Bed, so he could then pick up the shirt and put it over his head. We then worked through the following actions: Pick Up Bottom of Shirt, Head into Shirt, Arms Through Sleeves, Head Through Neck Opening. One could also set a tag point such as Pick up Next Clothing Item, to keep the momentum going until the task is finished. Tying shoes is a skill that lends itself particularly well to TAGteach, and there are many TAGteach videos on YouTube that demonstrate how to teach tying shoes. Although I describe this here as a sequential process, it will most likely be necessary to repeat each tag point a few times before moving to the next one.

Toileting is also a behavior chain that is often taught with a picture schedule; in addition, one could reinforce the picture schedule by setting the following tag points: Walks into Bathroom, Closes Door, Walks to Toilet, Pants Down, Sits on

Toilet, Goes, Uses Toilet Paper, Pants Up, Flush, Wash Hands. Actually, Wash Hands is its own behavior chain, with the tag points: Walk to Sink, Turn on Water, Get Soap, Soap on Hands, Rinse Hands, Put Soap Back, Turn Off Water, Dry Hands With Towel. Many autism families have varied and complex problems with toileting, so it is a topic that comes up frequently on the TAGteach Yahoo discussion group. Additional information is available in the archived posts and parents can review those for more specifics at www.tagteach.com.

Many children with autism dislike bathrooms for sensory reasons: the tile walls, running water and fixtures amplify and echo sounds, and it can be a hectic, cramped environment. To address this, I would work on making the bathroom an acceptable place: mark and reinforce the child for Walks Past Bathroom, Looks Into Bathroom, and Walks Into Bathroom. In this way I can shape the process of actually going happily into the bathroom. If the child likes water play, I would use that as a reinforcer for toileting activities.

We often had unpleasant bathroom behaviors pop up. The most annoying were excessive splashing in the sink and puddles of pee on the floor. To deal with these, I set the expectations of Dry Sink or Dry Floor. Technically these are not tag points because they are not physical movements of the child, rather they are the outcomes that I wanted. I found it difficult to come up with tag points for my child's behavior because I could not monitor him every time he went into the bathroom, so I settled on these outcomes as the next best thing. From then on, every time I noticed that the sink or floor was dry, I would call him over, praise him, and mark and reinforce. I had no way of knowing if it was dry because he was careful, or dry because he hadn't been in the bathroom for a while, but that didn't seem to matter. If there was puddle, I gave him a paper towel and gently indicated that he should help clean up, and I always thanked him for cleaning up. After a while, the sink and floor gradually had fewer puddles and more dry periods, and within a few weeks the puddles were gone. I still periodically point out and reward my son for Dry Sink and Dry Floor. Even when I could not reinforce my child at the exact moment he was doing what I wanted, the positive reinforcement helped build good behaviors.

Fine Motor Skills and Fun in the Tub

All children need good fine motor skills, especially for self-help (dressing and eating), play (manipulating toys) and learning (especially writing). Unfortunately many children nowadays have problems with fine motor skills, such as pinching, grasping and crossing the midline, not only our children on the autism spectrum. Crossing the midline is the ability to use both sides of the body and brain simultaneously. This is important for gross motor skills such as climbing stairs, walking, riding a bicycle and swimming. This section has some simple, inexpensive ideas for working on fine motor skills with a child during bath time using sponges, pouring toys, water bottles, and soap foam. I used all of these at home with my child. I haven't identified specific tag points for developing fine motor skills, but you could certainly apply the principles of shaping and TAGteach if your child has difficulty or needs more motivation than the water play itself provides.

Sponges: Buy some sponges with different shapes, sizes, colors, and especially textures. Some sponges have a very fine texture and others are coarse; be ready to experiment and see which kind the child likes best. Sponges that dry up to be very small and then expand dramatically in the water are also lots of fun. During the child's next bath, toss a sponge in the water and see what happens. Most likely, the child will pick it up and squeeze the water out of it. Encourage him to do this with the left hand as well as the right hand and also with both hands. Squeezing the sponges is an excellent fine motor activity. Work up from small sponges to larger sponges. As the sponges get larger, they become heavier when saturated with water, thus providing a little weight-bearing exercise. NOTE: Some of our kids have tactile defensiveness, so they may not like touching wet sponges. I would work up their tolerance as well as possible: put a sponge in the child's hand for just a moment, or try working with a washcloth for a while. During this time, I could use all kinds of language, for example, "Pick up the blue sponge," "Please give me that round sponge," "Here is a sponge that is shaped like a boat," and so forth; so the child can learn about colors, shapes and objects without realizing it.

Pouring Toys: Look for bath toys that encourage pouring activities: a little teapot set or measuring cups can work well for this. Encourage the child to pour water from the teapot into a cup. This is an excellent activity for grasping, hand-eye coordination, and crossing the mid-line. I would talk with my child about how many "pours" will fill a half-cup size or one-cup size measuring cup, and then I could quietly introduce the concepts of fractions and liquid measures.

Water bottles: Pick up some inexpensive spray bottles. Show the child how to unscrew the cap, fill the bottle with water, and screw the cap back on—this is very good for fine motor control and hand-eye coordination. Then the fun begins: have the child spray the water on the tub walls by squeezing the trigger. To make this activity even more fun, you can add the soap foam described next.

Soap Foam: Soap foam is generally available in the children's shampoo section. It comes in different colors and is inexpensive. Put globs of foam on the wall and have the child shoot them down with the spray bottle; most likely he will enjoy this. However, be forewarned: this soap foam is a challenging tactile substance and the child may dislike the feel of it. Doug hated this foam when I first brought it out. I placed gobs of it around the edge of the tub and he was so offended by it that he batted it into the water with his fingers as fast as he could. However, over time, he began to enjoy the sensation of this foam and it eventually became one of the highlights of bath time: he liked to shape it, squish it and pile it up.

So I found that bath time can be a great time to work on a child's fine motor skills. As always, experiment and adapt these suggestions to your personal situation. Be creative and persistent and you can use this recurring block of time to help the child develop those important fine motor skills.

Getting Along Around the House

It is easy to mark and reinforce a child for all kinds of good behaviors during the course of the day, and I found that I could spot all kinds of physical movements I liked. Here is a list of tag points that I worked on to help with getting along around the house:

- Eyes On Me
- Turns Head When Called
- Comes When Called
- Walks Toward Me

- Touches My Shoulder (precursor skill for asking for attention politely)
- Requests Food (toys, computer, activities, help, etc.)
- Eyes on Toy
- Hands on Toy
- Plays With Toy
- Eyes on Book
- Hands on Book
- Pages Through Book
- Sits on Chair
- Feet on Ground
- Two Steps in Same Direction (or Three Steps, Four Steps, etc.)
- Smiles
- Good Sound/Word
- Quiet Mouth
- Hands Still
- Feet Still
- Exhales
- Reacts to Environment (for example, looks at phone when it rings)
- Anything cute, clever, or creative!

Chapter 9
Play Skills

A helpful way to develop play skills is to set tag points relevant to the physical activity the child is working on. TAGteach, with its focus on reinforcing specific physical movements, is well-suited for this because play is various combinations of physical movements. When I want to teach my child to play with a certain toy or participate in a play activity, I review all the physical movements that are involved. See which ones Doug can already do and which ones he will need to learn. First I start marking and reinforcing him for the physical movements he can already do, strengthen those behaviors and put them on cue. Then I set tag points for the remaining behaviors and build those up.

Play With Toys

For teaching ball skills, potential tag points might be Looks At Ball, Walks Near Ball, Foot Touches Ball, Foot Pushes Ball, Hands on Ball, Drops Ball, Picks Up Ball, and so forth. For teaching a child to play with Legos or Lincoln Logs, the tag points might be Looks At Log, Touches Log, Picks Up Log, Places Log In Designated Spot. A key skill to work on in toy play is duration. After Doug could place one Lincoln Log, I marked and reinforced him for picking up a second and then a third. Doug went from being barely able to pick up a Lincoln Log to building towers and walls. I challenged him to "Do it one more time," and marked and reinforced him for playing longer. There are as many potential tag points as there are toys on the market, so study the toy you have selected, make sure the child can perform the actions required to play with the toy, model the play behaviors, and mark and reinforce the child for each play action. Use what you have learned in previous chapters about shaping (raising criteria in small steps toward the goal) and about designing effective tag points, based on the four tag point criteria:

1. What I Want
2. One Criterion
3. Observable
4. Five Words or Less

Luckily now there are many excellent technology products available, which have innumerable games, applications and other programs of interest. These can be very useful for a child with autism, and can be customized to the child's needs and interests. For example, Doug enjoys his computer, video and music programs, and they keep him happily occupied.

Here are some specific examples with instructions on how to teach bike riding and ball skills to children with autism.

Riding a Bike

Most of the teaching described in the previous sections focused purely on shaping. That is, raising criteria incrementally towards the goal behavior. Because Doug was unable to tolerate verbal instructions, I taught him without saying much and just allowed the click sound from the tagger to tell him "that was right, you get a treat!" I spelled out tag points for myself and explained them in detail in the above sections, but I did not use words to explain them to my son. In this section of the book on bike riding we will be moving away from the pure shaping that we have been discussing previously and will introduce the use of language in the TAGteach process for those of you who do want to describe the tag points for your children.

As Doug's receptive language skills improved, I was able to use more instruction and to use words to explain the tag points to him. I did not need to rely solely on shaping without words. For the bike riding example below, I introduce the concept of tag point phrasing. That is using words to explain the tag point. For example I could say, "The tag point is…Push Down" and then tag each time he pushes down on the pedals.

Bike riding is an important physical and social skill for all children, and especially for our special-needs kids. Some years ago I taught Doug to ride a bike. Here are some simple, inexpensive suggestions gleaned from our experience, for helping a child learn how to ride a bike, including wearing a helmet, pedaling skills, and balance. As always with autism, observe and monitor the child and make adaptations as necessary.

Helmets: Helmets are required safety gear for children in most states, and you can start teaching even a very young child to accept this headgear. Sometimes our special-needs children don't like the sensation and straps of a helmet, so I would start out by having a helmet in the toy box or play area. I would let the child become completely familiar with it and encourage him to put it on as much as possible. A helpful tag point is Helmet on Head. Also, I might go out and take some pictures of family members, friends and neighbors out on their bikes, scooters, skateboards and roller blades. Keep these pictures in a folder and bring out one or two during therapy or teaching sessions. I would show the picture to the child and say, "Look, there's Daddy riding his bike, and he's wearing his helmet. Let's put your helmet on your head." I would place the helmet on the child's head for a moment, mark, reinforce and move on. I would repeat this activity with pictures of other people and eventually I would have a pretty firm connection with the helmet and bikes or scooters.

Pedaling: Most children learn to pedal on their tricycles. We found a good tricycle and had Doug ride it (with a helmet on). To start, we needed to push his feet to get him to learn the motion of pedaling. Many tricycles now have a long handle attached so parents can push. As an extra cue, I put a large colored dots or stickers on each pedal. These types of visual cues are called targets, and they can be very useful in guiding hand and foot placement with all sorts of physical activities. I said to Doug, "Push down on the blue side, then push on the red side." Then say, "The tag point is...Push Down." I marked, reinforced, and praised him every time he pushed down on the pedals.

Balance: Balance skills are crucial for bike and scooter riding. The best way to develop these is just getting lots of physical activity for the child. I took advantage of the parks and playgrounds in our area, and Doug developed these abilities without realizing it. In wooded areas, the downed trees, log and stumps provide nature's balance beams, climbing towers and obstacle courses. For a younger child, simply walking along on an uneven mulched trail through the woods can be a good opportunity to learn balance skills.

Start with a Scooter: Once Doug had learned about helmets, pedaling and balance, we started working on the next step: riding a scooter. First we showed him how to push the scooter while walking. A tag point could be Hands on Handlebar. Next, we had Doug put one foot up on the running board and then encourage him to push with the other foot. Tag points for this activity were: Foot on Running Board, and Push With Foot. Two differently colored target stripes on the running board (made with marker on masking tape) gave cues as to exactly where to place his feet. You can say, "The tag point is…Foot to Red Stripe" if your child can understand this language. Even if you are not sure the child understands, you can say it anyway. We encouraged Doug to keep scootering and after some time, he learned to push and go. After Doug could push and move the scooter confidently, we encouraged him to get both feet on the running board and glide (again, using the two colored stripes as targets): the tag point is… Feet on Stripes. When he could consistently glide on the scooter for a distance of twenty to thirty yards with both feet on the running board, he was ready to move on to a bicycle.

Riding the Bike: It is important that the bike is light and on the small side; if the bike is too big, it will be difficult for the child to handle. We lowered the seat on the bike so that Doug could easily keep both feet flat on the ground while sitting. We didn't want him to be afraid if his feet couldn't touch the ground. Again, I started out by having him hold onto the handlebars and walk the bike. I used the same tag point as above: Hands on Handlebars. Then we got him to sit on the bike and push the bike with his feet (almost like a scooter), and said to him, "The tag point is…Push Down." Soon, Doug was able to get a foot up on the pedals (again, with colored dots or stickers on the pedals so he had those visual cues). At this point, I had to start running with the bike and holding on (no way to escape this). As with all children, it took him a while to get the trick of balancing on a bike, but with all our preparatory work, we weren't huffing and puffing along after him for too long!

Doug mastered riding a bicycle in just two weeks. This was the result of all the planning and preparatory work: he knew the helmet was mandatory, he knew how to pedal, and he was an expert glider on a scooter; we never used training wheels. He was very, very proud of riding that bike.

Ball Play

Several years ago I taught Doug to kick and bounce a ball. Here are some ways I did this. First, it helped to spend some time getting Doug used to the idea that the sight of Mom or Dad holding a ball is a good thing. As I went about my day, I carried a small ball with me, and whenever I gave Doug a little treat, I had him touch the ball before handing him the candy. Doug came to associate the ball with good things. Next, I took this process to the area where I planned to teach about the ball. I started initially just working in the yard or the driveway. I walked around with Doug and while I marked and reinforced him for other good behaviors, I kept having him touch the ball while I handed him a treat. After doing this for a while, I started working on ball skills. Several tag points are described below; you may not need to use all of them, or you may decide to create different ones. It all depends on the child's age and skill level, so adapt these suggestions to your specific situation.

Here is the shaping process I used to teach Doug to kick a ball. I set a large, light, colorful ball out in the yard. Every time he walked past the ball, I marked and reinforced! The initial tag point was Walks Near Ball. After a while he was walking right up to the ball, and whenever he was right by the ball, I marked and reinforced! The next tag point was Walks Toward Ball, and I marked and reinforced him for approaching the ball. Soon his foot brushed against the ball; from then on I marked and reinforced him only for brushing his foot against the ball; tag point was Foot Touches Ball. After a while, his foot actually pushed the ball, so I "raised the criteria" and marked and reinforced only for pushing the ball with his foot; the tag point was Foot Pushes Ball. At this point, it was easy to show him how to kick; I showed him how to do it, gave him the direction "kick the ball," and he did it very easily. He quickly understood how to walk up to the ball and give it a kick, and became pretty good at it. Once he was comfortable kicking, we set up a net and he could practice kicking the ball into the net.

For bouncing a ball, the procedure is similar. I started by having Doug hold the ball with both hands; the tag point was Hands on Ball. The next tag point was for him to Throw Ball; generally, the ball would bounce once and I would catch it. We played this easy catch game for a while with him throwing the ball to me while I caught it and either rolled it back to him or handed it to him (I didn't want to work on "catch" skills at that point). After a while, this became a fun activity for him and he started picking up the ball on his own and throwing it around.

Naturally, when playing with a ball, one starts to bounce the ball, so Doug often saw me bounce the ball and I would explain, "Look, I'm bouncing the ball." I bounced the ball gently towards him and asked him to bounce it back; the tag point was Hands Hit Ball. The next tag points were Hit Ball Down and Hit Ball Twice. At this point, I was able to say, "Let's see how often you can hit the ball," and we started counting the bounces. This was fun for both of us and he got lots of praise for more bounces. At first he could do only one or two bounces, but after more practice he was able to do more. Now he comfortably and confidently bounces the ball with both hands or with just one hand while running around the court.

A few more recommendations: in the beginning, work with a large, light, colorful ball so the child can easily kick it or hit it. Save the regulation soccer and basketballs for a later time. Practice only a few minutes at a time (not more than 10 or 15 minutes). Experiment with the tag points. The tag points listed above are the ones that worked for my son, but another child may need some intermediate tag points, or may be able to skip some. I am always careful to start my teaching plan at the level where Doug is able to do the movements; if the child can hold the ball, but cannot throw, build up his/her arm strength before asking the child to try to bounce the ball. For example, Doug was able to Hit Ball Down while it was moving towards him. Another child might need you to hold the ball in place so that he can then Hit Ball Down. Also, different children have different levels of verbal skills. Doug was younger when we worked on kicking, so that was more of a "shaping" activity. By the time we were working on bouncing, his receptive language skills were better so I could explain and demonstrate the tag points. As always, be aware of how your child is reacting to his environment and make whatever adaptations are necessary.

TAGteach is a wonderful, flexible method for teaching all kinds of physical skills to our children. It is quick, easy, and portable and can be adapted to whatever we are trying to do. Here is a summary of the process that I use: Look at the physical movement I want the child to make, break down the movement into steps that the child can do, then string the steps together. If Doug cannot do one of the steps, I break it down further or figure out a way to provide a support that will enable him to do the action. If your child has good receptive language skills, you can include more verbal instruction (but not too much talking!) and highlight the tag point by preceding it with the phrase, "The tag point is… [then the five words or less that describe the tag point]. If you child does not have good receptive language skills, or objects to verbal instructions, then you can teach any physical skill through shaping without words. Also, I find that teaching physical skills is fun and relaxing for me; I tend not to feel as driven as I do when working on those critical academic and communication skills, so this can be an enjoyable time with my child.

Chapter 10

Decreasing Disruptive Behavior and Increasing Calm Behavior

Tantrums

Even though autism parents do their best to avoid the obvious triggers of hunger, fatigue and sensory overload, all kinds of things can provoke a child with autism into a tantrum. On the very first day that I had a box clicker in my hand and treats in my pocket, I came downstairs and Doug, for no apparent reason, became enraged and started to shriek and jump. I was surprised because the morning had gone smoothly and there were no indications of any problems. Instantly, I started marking and reinforcing Quiet Mouth and Feet Still. Twelve minutes later he was sitting calmly and quietly on the sofa, looking at me with a stunned look on his face as though to ask, "How on earth did this happen?" From then on, I had a marvelous tool to deal with his tantrums.

To deal with tantrums, I use the following, now familiar, tag points:

- Quiet Mouth
- Hands Still
- Feet Still
- Exhales

Some years ago I encountered a phrase that always helps me when I have a problem. It is: "Difficult behaviors result from unmet needs." When Doug starts to tantrum, I check first to see if there is an obvious cause such as hunger, thirst, fatigue, illness, or too many or too difficult demands. For example, Doug has very specific needs to have food on a schedule; for Doug, hunger and anger are the same emotion. He can appear to be fine, but if he goes too long without food, it looks as though he has fallen off a cliff. It took me some time to understand that. Many of our tantrum problems went away after we set up a consistent food/snack schedule.

The demands placed on a child may be too much for him to handle: they may be too hard, too much, or too long for his behavioral and sensory levels. He may be experiencing little or no positive reinforcement and weak, ineffective supports. If so, he is probably experiencing high levels of failure and frustration and is at risk for tantrum behaviors. Also, our kids with autism have a lot of sensory issues. Tasks that might be fine for a typically developing kid can be very difficult for our kids because they are taking in so much more sensory input.

If people are aware of these reactions, it can be helpful to take them into account when planning the child's day. An immediate approach would be to change the balance of what a child is experiencing: from too much demand with too little reinforcement, to demands he can easily do plus lots of reinforcement and support. Over time, what I learned with Doug is that it is really bad to deliver a lot of failure and frustration. It is my job to make sure that he experiences success. When he experiences success he has truly magnificent behaviors. If he gets a big dose of failure and frustration, he gets really mad. Plus, the anger lasts for a long time. If he experiences failure and frustration at ten in the morning, he may still be angry at five in the evening. Again, you have the sensory issues: the negative emotions are experienced at very deep levels. I learned from my son how important it is to deliver success: the tasks he is given must be tasks he can do, plus he has to receive a lot of positive reinforcement for doing them. As he does the task more often, he can do it for longer periods of time and gradually take on harder tasks and do them for longer periods of time. It takes a lot of work to build desired behaviors in kids with autism: a lot of repetition and a lot of positive reinforcement. TAGteach is a great way both to increase the amount of positive reinforcement delivered to a child and to ensure that the child knows exactly why he is being reinforced. There is nothing else like it.

If there is no obvious cause, I sit down, say nothing, and wait for any Quiet Mouth, Hands Still or Feet Still behavior. I learned early on that Doug will have Quiet Mouth often because he has to stop screaming in order to inhale. I mark and reinforce those split seconds of Quiet Mouth. I also watch for Feet Still. Sometimes Doug was so upset that he rejected the treats. I learned not to worry about that, and set the treats on a table for later. As I marked and reinforced him for Quiet Mouth and Feet

Still, I started to feel calmer myself. I felt confident because I was focusing on my child's positive behaviors, *and* I had a strategy! There were many days when Doug was so difficult, and I was so worn out and tired that when a tantrum started, I felt ready to toss him out the window. (Note: I never did that.) The child's rage can make the parent feel enraged—a sad but understandable downward spiral. When the parent is angry and frustrated, it is difficult to deal calmly with the child's tantrum, but parents can clamp their mouths shut and start marking desired actions. Even when I was shaking with rage and frustration, I was able to keep marking and reinforcing good behaviors, and work on calming Doug down.

The huge benefit of marking and reinforcing desired actions during a tantrum is that both my child and *I myself* calmed down. Once I had more experience in using TAGteach to manage tantrums, I became less upset when a tantrum started. Doug realized that I was not upset, so he became less upset. Eventually I became totally calm and confident when a tantrum broke out, and that poise rubbed off on everyone around. I have been in situations when Doug blew up in public, and people around were taken aback. But since I was able to present such a cool, collected appearance, the onlookers relaxed and the tantrum petered out.

Transitions

Often children with autism don't like moving from one area or activity to another. A useful tag point for moving Doug along was Takes Next Step: mark and reinforce for taking the next step in the desired direction. Once the he was moving, I could mark and reinforce Walk Beside Me.

Since we haven't analyzed the four criteria for a tag point in a while, here it is again: in this case, an analysis of the tag point Takes Next Step:

1. **What I Want**: The child takes a step toward a new location or new activity.
2. **One Criterion:** Yes. Mark and reinforce the child when he Takes Next Step.
3. **Observable:** YES. I can see when the child has taken the next step. I could also count how many steps occurred in a period of five or ten minutes.
4. **Five Words or Less**: YES. Takes Next Step is three words.

The tag point Takes Next Step can be very useful in getting a child to go into new places. We once took Doug to visit some friends who had a wonderful basement recreation room, complete with pool table, a big sofa with soft, plushy cushions and other interesting things. I knew my son would have a great time down there, but was stymied by his refusal to go down the stairs. I set a tag point of One Step Down, waited with him at the top of the stairs, and marked and reinforced every instance of One Step Down. It took forty-five minutes, and many episodes of him going down a few steps and then racing back to the top, but finally he made a mad dash down the stairs and played happily in the room for the rest of the visit.

I generally find it helpful to give Doug a warning that a preferred activity will soon come to an end, and I have a treat ready when it is time to change. To the extent possible, I find it helpful to plan the day so that the things Doug does not like are followed by things the he does like: go to the store, then go to the playground. If the next item on the family schedule is not something the child likes, I explain, "After we do this, you can do that nice desired activity that you like." I mark and reinforce my child for any and all good and cooperative behaviors during the less desired activity, and then present the desired activity. Eventually, he experiences that change is okay and can become more flexible; the less desired thing wasn't so bad after all because he got lots of treats and praise for good behavior, and something better happened right after. It is important to note that Doug still receives lots of reinforcement during the less desirable (from his point of view) activity AND he gets the added reinforcement of the activity that he really likes afterward. It is not fair, and will not work, to expect a child to maintain a less desirable activity, with no reinforcement during that activity, with only the hope of earning the desirable activity. He may not even understand the connection and the logic that seems obvious to us.

Here's an example: say you explained to your child that if he walks nicely all the way across the parking lot, he will get to play on the swings. What happens if the nice walking only lasts half way across the parking lot? What do you do then? Do you have a struggle the rest of the way across and then he gets to play on the swings anyway, thus teaching the child that he can pretty much do what he wants because he knows you will give in? Do you go back (thereby ensuring a tantrum) because he didn't do the nice walking that would have earned him play time on the swings? Either way you lose and so does the child. The way I would accomplish the transition across the parking lot is to mark and reinforce Nice Walking frequently (or every step if necessary) and then have play time on the swings. This teaches the child that transitions aren't so bad and that even better things happen at the other end, and enables me always to keep my promise about the good things to come. This type of approach is particularly important if there are other children whose behavior is fine and who also want to play on the swings. It is not fair to them if they are taken home, because a sibling didn't meet the expectations for good behavior. In addition, denying all the children could result in the ever-popular double tantrum or triple tantrum as all they all join forces in protest.

So many things happen in family life that it is very helpful when a child with autism can cope with change. Even simple things like having to sit in a bigger car seat, switching rooms or changing the furniture can be upsetting, so it helps to have a strategy in place. When a change is imminent, no matter how minor it may seem to us, it can help to have a plan to make that change palatable to my child. I try to introduce the change in small increments. With the car seat example, I could place the new car seat in the living room and have the child practice sitting in it before I install it in the car (the tag point is…Sit in Car Seat). If I wish to rearrange my furniture, I might move one chair and let the child become accustomed to that: mark and reinforce the child for Eyes on Chair, Hands on Chair, Sits in Chair. I would slowly make other changes as necessary. I would have special treats ready, mark and reinforce my child for all good behaviors during the change period, and praise him for learning to accept the new situation. Doug seems to feel secure because he experiences support and positive reinforcement during change, and we parents feel confident because we can effectively manage the inevitable changes in family life.

At one point we replaced our ripped cloth sofa with a sturdy leather couch. We felt smug and confident that our son would not be able to poke his fingers into this one. Well, there was a surprise in store. I hadn't given any thought to preparing our son for this change. Our son hated the new sofa and figured out a clever way to take revenge: he couldn't poke holes or pull off the cushions and toss them on the floor, so he walked up to it and peed on it! Consternation! We howled with laughter, and immediately put in place a massive "love the new sofa" program. Every time he walked near the sofa, looked at the sofa, sat on the sofa, etc., we barraged him with candy, treats and praise. Now he perches happily on the sofa, lounges on it and even lies down on it occasionally.

Territorial Behavior

Sometimes as a child with autism approaches the teen years, he may exhibit territorial behavior. The child may not want people to be in a certain room, may want to have the room to himself, or may want to sit in a certain spot in the car. While this new bossiness can have its amusing aspects, it's not so funny if the child starts pushing people around. We had problems with this.

Our rule is: the parents provide the housing (or the car), so the parents are in charge. When my son entered his teens and started pushing me around, I simply put my hands on his arms and stated, "I am the Mom, so I am going to be in this room as long as I want to be here." This straightforward assertion caused him to back down. If a child wants privacy in his bedroom, that is appropriate and something to be encouraged, but the parents still have overall control of that room.

If Doug tried to insist, by pushing or pulling, that certain people be included or excluded from his presence, we asserted our right to determine who would be in the house, or who would go along on an outing. We made every effort to accommodate reasonable requests, but denied requests that were inappropriate or unsafe in our estimation. We also continuously marked and reinforced cooperative behavior. For us, the problem petered out.

At this point, when my son entered his teens, his receptive

language skills had increased to the point where he understood more words, but what worked best was my tone of voice. When he perceived that I was calm, yet determined to assert my rights, he reacted positively to that emotional information. Sometimes the emotional information embedded in the human voice is a great tool, and sometimes it is a hindrance. I learned from experience when to talk and when to tag.

Increasing Calm Behavior

In general, we all want our children with autism to be much calmer than they are. I was able to increase calm behaviors in my child by reinforcing the following tag points:

- Quiet Mouth
- Hands Still
- Feet Still
- Exhales

Initially I did this to get Doug to stop bouncing around constantly; then I ended up using it to build longer periods of calm, attentive behavior. Many children with autism are very tense, have high levels of physical agitation and anxiety, and spend a lot of time spinning, bouncing, jumping, and darting about. The non-stop action frequently upsets the parents. The sensitive, sensory child with autism quickly picks up on the parents' agitation and becomes more agitated in turn. Soon, everyone falls into a downward stress cycle. By marking and reinforcing calm behaviors, I was able to break this cycle.

I started with a five-minute observation of my son's physical agitation and noted the following physical movements: hands waving, feet off the floor (bouncing, jumping and running), squealing, giggling and other random sounds. I desperately wanted him to slow down and calm down. From the observation, I decided to reinforce the following behaviors, Quiet Mouth, Hands Still, and Feet Still. When he jumped up and went into action, I simply sat back, said not a word, and marked and reinforced any one of above behaviors. After a time, he was offering more Quiet Mouth, Hands Still and Feet Still behaviors. Then I "raised the criteria" and in order to receive the treat he had to be doing any two of the tag points at the same time. So, he had to be doing both Hands Still and Feet Still, for example, to earn the mark and reinforcement. Eventually he started offering combinations of two of the good behaviors. Then, I raised the criteria again, and he had to do all three tag points simultaneously to earn the mark and reinforcement. When he was able to do all three, I referred to this as "hitting the trifecta." One day, after he consistently had all three tag points going at the same time, he peered at me closely, walked over to his chair, sat down, folded his hands in his lap, and turned calmly toward me! I was thrilled. This process played out over a period of two to three months. From that point, he became much calmer and less physically disruptive. Naturally, the agitation would crop up now and again, but when it did, I sat back, started tagging the three tag points, and he calmed down quickly. For me, this was a wonderful experience of building a great behavior without using words.

After further observation and practice with this set of three tag points, I realized that another way my son displayed agitation was with quick, uneven breathing: I could even see the muscles in his throat pulsing. I started marking and reinforcing the exhalation of air; my tag point was Exhales. Very quickly his breathing relaxed and he became calmer. Surprisingly, as I was marking and reinforcing this tag point, I noticed that my breathing was becoming more relaxed and that I was calming down too. After about ten minutes, we were both quite relaxed. This, to me, was an unexpected and powerful demonstration of how the focus on marking and reinforcing a positive behavior built up a relaxation cycle, not only for the child, but for the parent as well. Sometimes unexpected opportunities presented themselves for dealing with behavior problems, and I was able to latch onto those and see what would happen.

Since the tag point Exhales was so useful, here is an analysis of the four criteria for the tag point:

1. **What I Want:** Child breathes calmly.
2. **One Criterion:** Yes. Exhales is a single physical movement.
3. **Observable:** YES. I can see and hear when the child exhales. I could also count how many times the child exhales during one minute.
4. **Five Words or Less:** YES. Exhales is one word.

Chapter 11

Self-Injurious Behaviors (SIB), Aggression, and Property Damage

Many children with autism exhibit self-injurious behavior: biting, hitting, scratching or poking at themselves, sometimes to the point of breaking the skin or causing physical harm. Or, they may hit, bite, kick, pinch and scratch people around them. These are devastating behaviors for parents to witness and extremely difficult to deal with. If your child exhibits these behaviors, consult with a Board Certified Behavior Analyst (BCBA) to set up a behavior management plan.

An excellent source of information about the function and treatment of self-injurious behaviors is the work of Dr. Brian

Iwata, Professor of Psychology and Psychiatry at the University of Florida. He is an internationally renowned expert on the analysis and treatment of severe behavior disorders.

Marking and reinforcing desired behaviors, along with other interventions, can play a helpful role in reducing these difficult behaviors. Marking and reinforcing the child as much as possible in the home can build new skills for the child and provide new insights for the parents (this is what happened to me). A child in a setting with high levels of positive reinforcement for desired behaviors can learn new skills, be more adaptable and have fewer outbursts. However, if and when the occasional aggressive or destructive outburst happens, we found it helpful to have a strategy for coping, discussed below. Please note that these are my personal thoughts on this situation and not recommendations for others. The best thing to do if a child displays aggression or self-injury, is to seek the help of a qualified professional. It would be so helpful if all autism families had access to such services, and the sad fact that we cannot get affordable, timely assistance for these horrible, heartbreaking situations is one of the tragedies of life with autism.

My child displayed aggression in the early years and over time we developed a set of rules for him.

Rule #1: You are not allowed to hurt people.

Rule #2: You are not allowed to destroy property.

Rule #3: If you make a mess, you are responsible for cleaning it up (or at least helping).

I also developed a set of rules for myself:

Rule #1: Only ask him to do what he is capable of doing.

Rule #2: Only ask him to do something for the length of time that he is capable of doing it.

Rule #3: Monitor his emotional reactions carefully.

Rule #4: Mark and reinforce lavishly all good behaviors.

Rule #5: Give a treat every time I mark a behavior (regardless of whatever subsequent behavior is occurring)

Sometimes my child became aggressive during a tantrum, and sometimes the aggression seemed to come from nowhere. For a while, when Doug first woke up in the morning and came downstairs he would walk over to me and punch me on the arm. Why, I have no idea, but I was extremely upset and angry. Eventually I learned to do the following: Immediately after the first punch, I held his hands down and gently said, "It's okay to be mad, and I'm sorry you are upset, but you may not hit (bite, kick, pinch, punch or spit at) people. If you are upset, say 'Help,' or 'Mad' and I will help you." Generally this straightforward assertion of Rule #1 would calm him down. Whether he understood all the words, I cannot say for sure, but he understood the tone of voice. I was calm and determined. He sensed that and reacted accordingly. If he continued to be upset I marked and reinforced all possible Quiet Mouth, Hands Still, Feet Still and Exhales until he calmed down.

I followed the same procedure for damage to property in the home. For destructive behavior, I pulled my child away and said calmly and gently, "I'm sorry you feel mad and upset. It's okay to have those feelings, but you may not damage property (kick the walls, punch holes in things, tear up pillows, break things). If you feel really angry, say 'Help' or 'Mad' and I will help you." Again, the assertion often calmed my child. When it did not, I marked and reinforced all possible Quiet Mouth, Hands Still, Feet Still and Exhales moments. After he recovered, he had to help clean up. I told him, "The rule is, if you make a mess, you have to clean it up." He had to pick up, even if it was only one or two things, put them back or use a paper towel to clean up. Naturally I marked and reinforced all cooperative behaviors. While this may be fine for the occasional episode, if your child has severe levels of property destruction, seek the help of a qualified professional.

I eventually realized that I was part of the problem. For a long time, I was an insensitive clod, focusing on the learning goals I had in mind instead of my child's reactions. I often pushed him beyond his limits, with the result that he exhibited aggression and rage. It took me a long time to appreciate the devastating impact of demanding too much for too long. (Who's the slow one now? After all, I was convinced I was "doing what was best" for him.) I finally realized it one day when, after a violent outburst during a series of tasks that were too difficult for him, he was still profoundly upset six hours later. Dumb. It took me a long time to appreciate how much my child wanted to please, and how proud he was when he was able to do something well. Again, dumb. I failed to appreciate how important it is to set a task at the level the child can perform (i.e., failed to have him start at the "point of success"). Now I strictly follow my first rule: only ask him to do what he is capable of doing. This can vary from day to day, so I am always willing to start a few steps back from where I left off if I need to. I know that I will be able to move quickly back to where I was, and without frustration.

Then, after he failed, I kept having him do it over and over.

I failed to pay attention to his endurance limitations; I violated the "three try rule." This is a guideline that says, if the learner fails to perform the tag point after three attempts, the instructor should step back, re-think the situation and devise a new, achievable tag point. Like all humans, my son craves success. When he experienced failure (imposed by me), he got mad. If he kept experiencing failure again and again he got even madder. It took me a long time to learn *from him* that my job is to set up his tasks so that he has success, and to respect his endurance limitations. Now I strictly follow my second rule: only ask him to do something for the length of time that he is capable of doing it.

It also took me a long time to learn to read his stress signals and react to them. If I ignored the warning signals (cheeks sucked in, angry noises) and pressed on, he revolted. Rightly so. That was Rule #3: Monitor his emotional reactions carefully. Life is much better now that I know, in detail, how to read his stress signals, how to build up his skills in such small increments that he experiences success, and how to build up his endurance. Finally, Rule #4: I mark, reinforce, praise and thank him for his effort and other good behaviors. Putting these practices into place changed everything for the better. His aggressive behaviors dropped dramatically, and now the highlight of his day is his academic sessions. He can't wait to get started and often sits patiently at the table waiting for me.

More of my personal thoughts: since aggression and destruction may result from stresses in the child's environment, it is important to be aware of anything that is going on that could agitate the child. While it is impossible to remove all stresses from the life of any human, it can be helpful to remember that new, unexpected or difficult demands placed on a child with autism can spark tantrums and violent behaviors. Just as our children are extremely sensitive to sensory stimuli, they can be equally sensitive to the level of demand that is placed upon them, and the duration of that demand. If a child experiences high, difficult demand levels for long duration with low reinforcement, and that stress is repeated day after day, the child may become more and more agitated, with all kinds of dreadful behavioral outcomes.

My personal belief is that the adults in the life of a child with autism have a duty to make sure that the child can perform the tasks he is asked to do, for the length of time required, and that the child is reinforced for his/her efforts and accomplishments. If you have a child like mine, whose behaviors in the early days consisted solely of screaming, stomping, spinning and bouncing, then you have to work up from there; you cannot expect such a child to sit still and cooperate with an instructional session, no matter how well intentioned.

In those early days, I held my bouncing, wildly distracted child down on the chair and tried to get him to touch blocks and point to pictures, while offering treats and blowing bubbles. If I could do it over with the knowledge I have now, I would mark and reinforce intensively all Quiet Mouth and Hands/Feet Still moments to get him calmed down, then mark and reinforce to build up Nice Sitting, build endurance for Sit at Table, and finally work up from there to other learning behaviors. Initially this will be a slow, tedious process, but once the child gets going, realizes he is learning, and realizes that he can trust his environment, things can move along more smoothly.

While it is important that our children with autism learn the rules of society (we cannot hurt people or destroy property, and we are responsible for our messes), it is my belief that everyone involved with the child accept the profound responsibility to recognize and honor the burden that autism places upon the child in terms of learning and behavior. If the child cannot do something or avoids doing something, no matter how commonplace or trivial the task may appear to us (or even if the child was able to do it the day before), there is no choice to be made about what we should do or what we should not do: we *must* accept that … and start thinking about how to make it possible for the child to do the task. We should think about the components of the task and whether the child knows all the components, and we should think about the endurance required to complete the task. It is our responsibility to make sure the child can do all the steps in the task without experiencing failure or fatigue. This requires vigilant observation and the ability and willingness to adapt in response to the child's behavior. It is our responsibility to teach and support our child in the most humane, effective way possible, even though we must accept in our hearts that it will take a long time and a lot of repetition.

Chapter 12

Teaching the Babysitter

Autism parents need a break, but it can be very difficult to find babysitters or even family members who are willing to watch and capable of watching a child with autism. TAGteach can be a wonderful way to make a tough job easier, because even a ten-year old can learn to mark and reinforce behaviors pretty quickly. Invite some potential baby sitters over to the house, either family members, friends, or teenagers in the neighborhood; having two at a time come over to work with a child would be ideal, plus they can be companions for each other. Invite them to the house for just an hour to start and give them a brief explanation of marking and reinforcing physical movements. Give each person a box clicker and a few treats and ask them to watch for, then mark and reinforce, each moment of Hands Still or Feet on Ground. Once they have some experience, give them a list of other tag points you are working on. You can even mark and reinforce the helpers for tagging your child!

Often, when people have some experience they catch on to TAGteach quickly and really enjoy it. After they have marked and reinforced the child a few times, you can ask them to mark anything the child does that they think is good, then wait and see what they come up with. You may hear all kinds of interesting observations. Best of all, everybody will have fun. After a series of practice sessions with TAGteach-savvy helpers, the parents can take a short break and leave their child in safe, enthusiastic and capable hands.

Chapter 13

Summary of the TAGteach Approach

Summary of the Procedure for Applying TAGteach

The TAGteach process is: Identify, Mark, Reinforce.

- Start by observing the child's behaviors.
- Identify the physical movements the child makes with his body to do the behaviors.
- Decide what movements you would like the child to make and set tag points according to the four criteria of:
    1. What I Want
    2. One Criterion
    3. Observable
    4. Five Words or Less

- Start at the "point of success," that is, a physical action that the child can already perform.
- Mark and reinforce the child whenever he performs the tag point. Observe the child's reactions and adjust the tag point accordingly. If the child cannot perform the tag point after three tries, re-assess and make changes.
- In the early stages, mark and reinforce every single instance of the tag point to the greatest extent possible. Praise and encourage the child.
- Work in short sessions and watch the child for signs of stress, boredom or distractedness. End on a high note and know when to stop. Avoid the temptation for "just one more."
- Think about whether you are: in the "building" stage of developing this behavior or the "maintenance" stage. Start with "building," and when you feel the behavior is strong, switch to "maintenance" and reinforce it on a variable schedule.

Point of Success

Set the first tag point as something the child can do and where he is guaranteed to be marked and reinforced.

Three Try Guideline for Tag Points

If a child fails to perform the designated tag point after three tries, the parent should analyze the situation and devise a more achievable tag point. The three-try "rule" is actually more of a guide than a rule. Some children want to work things out for themselves and will try several times without becoming discouraged. Others would rather take very small steps forward and experience success each time. The important responsibility is to be familiar with your child and respect his needs.

My TAGteach Guidelines Checklist

- ☑ Use the tagger as a signal to my child when I LIKE a behavior he is doing.
- ☑ Tag on time.
- ☑ Give a treat or other reinforcer for every tag (one tag/one reinforcer).
- ☑ Tag often (2-5 times a minute or more during tag sessions).
- ☑ Ignore mistakes and never give orders, yell, scold or criticize while using the tagger.

Chapter 14

Questions and Answers

How will the child know that the event marker means anything?

There is a quick process sometimes referred to as "charging" the clicker. Before I started marking and reinforcing my child for a behavior, I sat down near him and practiced pressing the clicker and handing him a little treat after each click. I did this rapidly and steadily for a minute or two. My son figured out in about twenty-five seconds that the mark meant that a treat was coming, and then he started to watch out for it. Learning something new in 25 seconds is pretty fast learning.

How will the child know what the tag point is?

Highly intelligent, verbally skilled children and adults learn quickly with TAGteach; the verbal instruction, "The tag point is…" provides simple, clear instructions, and the mark/reinforce process tells them instantly whether they have achieved success. You can also model or demonstrate the desired behavior. Modeling is a powerful teaching tool. Or, switch places: give the clicker to the child and ask him to mark you for doing the desired task. This can be great fun and very empowering for the child.

If the child is non-verbal, you can demonstrate the tag point. I find that I rarely need to describe the tag point verbally because my child is supremely capable of figuring out how his environment is changing. In fact, in our case, using words in the early years to describe a desired movement was actually counterproductive. I believe that our kids with autism are much more perceptive than we are. They are keenly aware of their environment and, like all humans, are constantly seeking information and reinforcement. If you start marking and reinforcing Hands Still, they experience that their environment is rewarding them for Hands Still and not rewarding them for Flapping Hands; they figure out quickly that Hands Still is the behavior to do. That is the beauty of TAGteach: it works as well for the nonverbal child as for the verbal child, because it plays to the child's strengths: his high level of sensory awareness.

Should I explain the tag point?

Generally, long explanations are not recommended. A tag point should be a single muscle movement that can be described in just a few words. If you have to explain, then the tag point may be too complex. Review the four tag point criteria described in earlier chapters and break down the desired behavior further. You can then describe the tag point to a verbal child or model it for a nonverbal child. For example, you could put your hands on the grocery cart and say to your child "Do this." With the verbal child you could say: "The tag point is hands on bar". But often it's not necessary. We adults are much too enamored of our words, our language and our explanations. We need to keep it simple, keep our own mouths quiet, and let the clicker do the talking.

I'm nervous about marking and reinforcing a child. Is there any way I can practice first?

Yes. It is easy to practice marking and reinforcing specific muscle movements. All you need is another person to be present. Ask your helper to walk slowly around the room, and practice marking Right Foot on Floor. Every time the helper takes a step and his/her right foot hits the floor, press the clicker. Switch to Left Foot on Floor. You can also sit next to the helper and mark eye blinks; that is more random than walking and is a bit more challenging. Ask your helper to bounce a big ball on the floor. You can mark Hands on Ball or Right Hand on Ball.

Where should I do this?

The beauty of TAGteach is that you can do it in anywhere: the house, the yard, the playground, the car, the bus, the doctor's office. It is light, portable, and flexible. I found that it expanded the number of settings in which my child could learn new skills.

How do you deal with marking and reinforcing in public?

I have been marking and reinforcing my child in public for years, and have had only two or three questions in that entire time. I found out that people are so preoccupied with their own needs and their own schedules that they rarely observe what is going on around them. Also, many of the environments where we spend time are noisy. If you are marking and reinforcing a child in the grocery store, then you are already in a noisy environment with music, carts rolling, kids running around, and machinery operating. Even if people hear the click, they will probably assume it is some piece of equipment in the store. If you are in an outside environment, they will assume it is a passing car or construction vehicle.

In case of questions, though, I have two responses. If an adult asks me what I am doing, I say, "I'm using positive reinforcement with an event marker signal to teach my child a skill." This usually renders the person speechless. If they are interested and ask more questions, I explain. If a child asks me (and children are more likely to inquire), I say, "I give my son a tag when he does something good, and now I'm going to give you a click because you asked a good question!" I immediately tag the children and they always run off with happy faces.

What treats should I use?

Treats, or reinforcers, are anything that the child enjoys and would like to get more of. Treats are frequently candy. Since you have to hand out treats many times in the course of the day, I recommend small pieces of candy that are easy to carry in your pocket, and easy and quick to hand to the child. I had great success for years with long strips of fruit rolls: it was easy to tear off a tiny sliver and hand it to my child, and he loved it. I could go all day and use only two fruit rolls, so he did not get too much. Pretzels, cereal, and any candy that can be broken into tiny pieces work well. Avoid candies that are chewy, sticky or long-lasting; you want the child to get the treat, eat it quickly, and be ready for the next treat. The most important factor is that the pieces are small and easy to handle. Some people may object to the idea of giving a child candy for health reasons, but honestly, I had much bigger problems to deal with.

In place of candy, many people like to use tokens or tickets for treats. The child can accumulate tokens and tickets and trade them in for trinkets in a treasure box, special privileges (a movie or pizza dinner) or for money. Use whatever system is reinforcing for your child. There are many catalog companies that sell token systems. The TAGteach website offers "tagulators." A tagulator is a set of beads on a plastic string. Every time the child earns a tag, he can pull a bead down the string. After ten or twenty beads are pulled down, the child earns a treat or a token; the act of pulling down the bead is very reinforcing in itself.

Sometimes older children aren't interested in candy or trinkets, but they may like computer games, the Wii or other devices. If your child is spellbound by computer devices, you have an excellent opportunity to use access to these devices as a reinforcer. First you need to assert control over your child's access to the computer, TV, Wii, iPad, or whatever device the child wants. Then, you can set criteria and require the child to do tasks to earn access privileges. Set up a token system whereby the child earns 10 minutes of computer time for each homework assignment, household chore, or cooperative task. You can organize the token system in whatever way works best for your family situation, but the key points are that the child has to perform specified behaviors in return for specified minutes of access, and the child cannot have access to the device until he has completed the tasks and earned the tokens. Devising clever, effective reinforcement is a true skill and a very valuable one.

What to do if a behavior weakens?

If you see that a desired behavior has dropped out of a child's repertoire, or he isn't doing it as well or for as long a time, start over with the original tag points. Mark and reinforce every instance of the desired behavior, build it back up, and then work on maintenance. Since the child already knows how to do the behavior, patching it up should go fairly quickly.

How long to do TAGteach?

This depends on what you are working on and how much time is available to the family. TAGteach can be intensive in that you set aside a time and place and work on a behavior, or it can be casual in that you go about with the child and mark and reinforce every time he does something you like. When I was teaching Nice Walking, I set aside regular times to build that behavior. When we are home, I mark and reinforce desired behaviors during the course of the day, looking for and rewarding any behaviors that I like. If you are doing intensive teaching, several sessions per day of ten to twenty minutes each would be ideal. If you are doing casual teaching, you can do it anytime and anywhere. TAGteach is easy to incorporate into the daily routine. My clicker is attached to my belt so I always have it handy, and I always keep a few treats in my pocket. This way, I am "armed and ready" to deal with behaviors in any situation.

What about tagging too soon (or too late)?

When you start thinking about whether you are marking a tag point too soon or too late, then you are an accomplished TAGteacher! If you mark too soon or too late, give the child the treat; the rule is, if you mark the behavior, you must give reinforcement. The goal of the tag point is to mark a specific muscle movement that you want the child to do more often. Sometimes when you watch the child, you think he is about to do the movement and you mark, but then the child doesn't do it. This happens to me every now and then. It doesn't matter. Just give the child the treat, and wait for the next opportunity. The same goes for marking too late. These little errors crop up for everyone, but luckily, I have found that the mark/reinforce process is forgiving, and a few incorrect marks will hurt nothing.

My child stopped doing the behavior. What happened?

In the early stages of learning, a child may stop performing a behavior after it has been marked. This is to be expected, because you are teaching a new behavior and it takes a while for it to become stronger and more reliable. Just keep watching and you will see the behavior pop up again. Patience and persistence will build the behaviors you want.

Do I have to give a treat every time I mark a behavior? What if the child is doing something that I don't like right after he hears the marker sound?

Yes, you do have to give a treat every time you mark. The marker sound is a promise that a treat will come. The marker sound will become very important to your child, and you cannot break your promise, even if you don't manage to give the treat quickly enough.

Will TAGteach work if my child is extremely wild and totally unmanageable?

This is precisely the situation where TAGteach can be very helpful. When you see children with autism who display extraordinarily wild and chaotic physical behaviors, it can look like there is no place to start. The important point to remember is that all behavior is variable. At some split second, that screaming, twisting child will have a micro-second of Quiet Voice or Hands/ Feet Still or Both Feet on Ground. Those microseconds are the perfect places to begin. Mark and reinforce those behaviors intensively. Look for every possible opportunity to tag anything that is remotely "good." The child will start to do more of those behaviors. We have all seen children (or seen videos of children) with autism who are bouncing, spinning and shrieking so badly that it breaks your heart to watch. These children are suffering and so are their families. But in those videos, I also spotted microseconds of Quiet Mouth or Hands Still that could be marked and reinforced. No matter how fleeting the "good" behavior is, intensive marking and reinforcement can make that behavior occur more often, so even during those horribly disorienting times, it is worth the time and effort to set the tag points, help the child, and alleviate the suffering.

Chapter 15

Reforming the Future with TAGteach

"I wish I knew how to reach my child."

"How can I get through to him?"

"There is so much in there. I just wish I could get it out."

Many autism parents have thought and said these words. I believe that TAGteach gives families a simple, inexpensive way to reach and teach their children with autism. It helped us tremendously.

The event marker and the positive reinforcement that follows can pinpoint and strengthen desired behaviors. Life is better when we can take our children out, go places without tantrums, and lead a more normal life. It is not a replacement for other methods of teaching a child with autism. It will not cure autism. But it can be extremely helpful.

The home is not the only place where TAGteach can make improvements. Schools, adult daytime work sites, and residential placements are also places where TAGteach can make a contribution. My vision is that in any place where there are children or adults with autism, the instructors and aides are equipped with clickers and treats and have posted lists of constantly evolving tag points for each individual. My vision is that when an individual performs one of the tag points, all hands reach out, a chorus of clicks marks the behavior for the individual, and treats and praise are showered on that person. My vision is that individuals with autism will learn new skills, and their instructors and aides will experience the pride and thrill of successfully teaching their charges. What a great way to manage, teach and train. Talk about empowerment!

There is so much at stake for our children with autism. Doug is now a teenager, and like many parents, we worry about his life as an adult when he will have to live in some type of facility. Like all autism parents, we want him to be safe, secure and protected; we do not want him to be punished for displaying behaviors that are due to his autism. There are, sadly, all too many accounts of children and adults with developmental disabilities who are being punished or brutalized in such facilities. There is no excuse for such treatment when we have scientifically-based methods of behavior management, and with an application like TAGteach, we have a simple, inexpensive way to mark, reinforce and build good behaviors.

So let's change this picture. The obvious solution is a system of positive behavioral supports that is easy to implement. The beauty of TAGteach is that it is simple and easy to do. If the child or adult is doing something or anything that is "good," just mark and reinforce. If the child or adult is upset, start tagging Quiet Mouth, Hands Still, Feet Still, or Exhales; and get that person calmed down. Let's abolish the use of coercion, verbal abuse and physical force with human beings who have developmental disabilities. Let's use our knowledge and bring out the best in our children and adults with autism, and bring out the best in their caregivers.

Recently, I pulled up to a red light, happened to glance at the car on the right, and noticed a young man with autism in the back seat. He was rocking rhythmically back and forth, never missing a beat, never looking to left or right, with his face and mouth frozen into an odd grimace.

This young man was clean, well groomed and nicely dressed. Obviously his caring family had made arrangements for him to be taken somewhere, but he was as imprisoned by his behaviors as if he were draped in chains. What a loss.

But what an opportunity. Think about the benefits of a system that tackles these behaviors, reduces the repetitive movements and builds new, functional and happy behaviors. What kind of charming person might emerge? How powerful would we be as a society to lift this young man, and the millions like him, to a much more meaningful level of life?

Here is the challenge. Let's get to work.

Made in the USA
San Bernardino, CA
20 September 2016